BUILD A BETTER YOU —STARTING NOW!

BUILD A BETTER YOU –STARTING NOW!
6

CORINNE A. KRAUSE, Ph.D.
Dr. H. PAUL JACOBI
DOROTHY JONGEWARD, Ph.D.
MARIA ARAPAKIS
MARILYNN NIXON
DICK and GLORIA COBB
NICOLE SCHAPIRO
BILL MEYER
JACK H. GROSSMAN, Ph.D.
CHERIE CARTER-SCOTT
EDWARD E. SCANNELL
FRANCES MERITT STERN, Ph.D.
HOWARD W. BONNELL
Dr. RICHARD BENCE

DONALD M. DIBLE, Series Editor
CAROL FOREMAN BROCKFIELD, Senior Staff Editor

SHOWCASE PUBLISHING COMPANY
Fairfield, California

Library of Congress Catalog No. 79-63064
ISBN 0-88205-205-5

Printed in the United States of America.

Showcase Publishing Company
3422 Astoria Circle
Fairfield, California 94533

Distributed to the retail trade by
Elsevier-Dutton, Inc., New York

First Printing

TABLE OF CONTENTS

PREFACE - vii
Donald M. Dible, Series Editor

1 - FACE THE FUTURE WITH A SMILE - 1
Corinne A. Krause, Ph.D.

2 - TO BE OR NOT TO BE... DIFFERENT - 17
Dr. H. Paul Jacobi

3 - STOP PLAYING THOSE GAMES! - 33
Dorothy Jongeward, Ph.D.

4 - SETTING LIMITS:
THE ART OF SAYING NO - 57
Maria Arapakis

5 - MAKE ROOM FOR JOY - 79
Marilynn Nixon

6 - HOW TO LOVE BEING MARRIED - 95
Dick and Gloria Cobb

7 - THE AMERICAN DREAM:
FREEDOM THROUGH COMMITMENT - 111
Nicole Schapiro

8 - PLAY YOUR OWN HANDICAP - 131
Bill Meyer

9 - IT'S JUST UNCOMMON SENSE - 145
Jack H. Grossman, Ph.D.

10 - BUILDING THAT PIONEER SPIRIT - 161
Cherie Carter-Scott

11 - I KNOW YOU <u>THINK</u>
YOU UNDERSTAND WHAT I MEANT - 177
Edward E. Scannell

12 - STRESS AND HOW TO COPE WITH IT - 197
Frances Meritt Stern, Ph.D.

13 - THE HAZARDS OF AVERAGE THINKING - 211
Howard W. Bonnell

14 - I CAN DO IT! - 225
Dr. Richard Bence

INTRODUCING THE SERIES EDITOR - 241

PREFACE

Hello. We at the Showcase Publishing Company are truly delighted to be able to bring you this sixth volume in our series *Build a Better You—Starting Now!* I'd like to use this opportunity to tell you just a little bit about this volume, this series, and our publishing company.

First, a word about this volume. Here you have the opportunity to benefit from the motivating, inspiring, and enthusiasm-generating ideas of 14 of North America's most exciting platform personalities—speakers whose messages are heard in person or on cassette by hundreds of thousands of people every year. Now you have the opportunity to read transcripts of their most popular talks and share their most carefully thought-out ideas and discoveries as they commit their observations to the printed page. These messages are now available for the first time in book form. *Build a Better You—Starting Now! Volume 6* is that book—the sixth in a planned series of 26 volumes.

Next, a word about this series. A full year of motivational, inspirational and self-help "vitamins."—that's the idea behind this 14-chapters-per-volume, 26-volume series. That's a full year's supply of mental nourishment to be consumed at the rate of one chapter per day for 365 days. (Volume 26 will contain 15 chapters, for a total of 365 chapters.)

Drawing from the best of the tens of thousands of established and fast-rising stars in the self-help speaking field, this series is dedicated to bringing to wider-and-wider audiences throughout the world a vital message: *You can build a better you—starting now!* If you are truly dedicated, you can make it happen.

Finally, a word about the Showcase Publishing Company. Showcase was launched by the founders of The Entrepreneur Press, a nine-year-old company dedicated to publishing books for new and small business owners. (One of our titles, *Up Your OWN Organization!—A Handbook on How to Start and Finance a New Business,* has sold more than 100,000 copies.) All of the customers of The Entrepreneur Press are interested in self-help information. However, as we came to appreciate that a far larger audience existed for self-help information directed at personal development, the decision was made to start a new company dedicated to serving this larger audience.

As a public speaker myself (I regularly present more than 100 seminars a year), and as a member of several associations of public speakers, I realized that my fellow speakers could provide an enormous amount of material for the new audience we had chosen to serve. It was at this point that we decided to start Showcase. We sincerely hope you will agree that we did the right thing.

DONALD M. DIBLE
Publisher and Series Editor
SHOWCASE PUBLISHING COMPANY
3422 Astoria Circle
Fairfield, California 94533

BUILD A BETTER YOU —STARTING NOW!

CORINNE A. KRAUSE, Ph.D.

Corinne Krause successfully combines family and profession in her own life. The wife of a physician and the mother of four children, she was an active community volunteer before returning to school to teach at Carnegie-Mellon University and earn her doctorate in history. As a consultant and seminar leader for managers, spouses, and office workers, Corinne combines lessons from history with her own experience to build understanding of traditional women's roles, current trends, and future challenges. Corinne believes and teaches that understanding and determined effort can assure success.

Corinne's interest in how women have managed multiple responsibilities throughout history led her to organize a group of women to tape-record 225 oral history interviews with three generations of women. Her seminar "Grandmothers, Mothers, and Daughters," and the videotaped group interview "Seventy-Seven—And Still Going Strong" delight and instruct male and female audiences about women who juggle family, work, and community commitments.

Corinne's newest seminar focuses on women today as they face the dual responsibility of family and work. Her positive approach to this central issue of the 1980s builds confidence and motivation among women and encourages corporate managers to make the most of the valuable human resource that family women represent.

In addition to many published articles, Corinne is the author of *How to Up Your Potassium*, a low-salt, low-cholesterol cookbook which she wrote in response to her mother's special diet needs. Corinne is also the proprietor of The History Company, which specializes in organizational histories and oral history.

She is listed in *Who's Who of American Women* and *Who's Who in the East.*

You may contact Corinne by writing to P. O. Box 81096, Pittsburg, PA 15217. Telephone (412) 521-4466.

FACE THE FUTURE WITH A SMILE

by CORINNE A. KRAUSE, Ph.D.

Close your eyes for a moment and think about the three happiest times of your life. Ninety-nine chances out of a hundred, at least one of them will be connected with family.

From the time we are born, family is central to our fulfillment and happiness. This is true for all of us, male or female, single or married. In spite of high divorce rates and changing life styles, family continues to be an important part of our lives. In fact, one of the great contemporary challenges is to find a balance between one's needs as an individual and as a family member. This is a particular problem for women.

3

Old Values — New Realities

Families come in many different shapes. We are all familiar with the textbook American family as it has been pictured on television and in primary-grade readers. Dad works and Mother keeps house, cooks, and cares for two or three children and a dog named Spot. Today this family is not typical; in fact only 7 percent of American families fit this pattern.

Each year more and more women enter the work force, and the result is that most of us have two jobs. Our unpaid job begins early in the day and often resumes in the evening hours. We did not plan this lifestyle; when we were growing up most of us did not expect to work after marriage. I know that I was raised with the sole thought of becoming a wife and mother. Nothing in my background prepared me for a lifetime career, and I even felt a sense of guilt when I accepted my first teaching position as a married woman.

Parents and teachers used to treat girls differently from boys. At school girls were taught to value achievement, yet at the same time were given the message that they should not be quite as smart as the boys. Good grades were nice, but girls were expected to be modest about their achievements. Most of us tried to live up to the expectations of the people around us.

Well society has changed and women are playing a major part in the change. As a result we now find ourselves with old values and new realities. We now face the challenge of combining family goals with our ambitions for personal fulfillment. I am convinced that women have within themselves the power to combine the two to create a truly full and satisfying life. The range of possibilities has increased dramatically, and we know that the choice is ours. But choice can be frightening. We sometimes wonder, "Can I do it?"

Those of us who have confidence that what we want is right and good will be successful at integrating the goals of individual accomplishment and family. For others it may be difficult. Many of us are inhibited by a voice deep within us that says we should be totally satisfied through our families alone. We must free ourselves from this constricting conditioning.

Working to Help the Family: A Bit of History

When we look back in history we learn a great deal about women, work, and families. The Bible teaches us that dual responsibilities are not at all new. The Book of Proverbs describes a "good wife" whose worth is "far above rubies":

> . . . *She seeks out wool and flax and works*
>   *willingly with her hands . . .*
> *She rises while it is yet night, and gives food*
>   *to her household . . .*
> *She considereth a field and buys it;*
> *With her earnings she plants a vineyard.*
> *She girds herself with strength and braces her*
>   *arms for work.*
> *She finds that her trade is profitable;*
> *Her lamp goes not out at night . . .*
> *She sets her hand to the distaff;*
> *Her fingers hold the spindle.*
> *She stretches out her arms to the needy . . .*
> *She makes her own tapestries . . .*
> *She makes linen cloth and sells it;*
> *She supplies the merchants with girdles.*
> *Dignity and honor are her garb,*
> *She looks to the future with a smile.*
>
> —Proverbs 31:10-31

The Bible offers a role model to women of today, for the "woman of valor" fulfilled the double role of nurturing homemaker and breadwinner. I recently had the fascinating experience of directing a study of the history of twentieth-century women, and the results indicated the continuation of this ancient tradition.

The idea for my research grew out of the frustrations of trying to teach a history without women. As a professor at Carnegie-Mellon University I searched for materials about women to incorporate into my classes, but published material about women was scarce. History was written about men.

Research was needed to bring women into the mainstream of history, and an exciting seminar convinced me that tape-recorded oral history interviews would effectively preserve the lifestyles, roles, and attitudes experienced by women of different ages over the course of the century. The result was an oral history study of three generations of women.

In the course of my research, more than 200 women of different ages and ethnic backgrounds tape-recorded information about themselves, their families, and their work. Most of these women were raised in traditional homes with traditional values. For every one of them, family responsibility held top priority. And many of the older women had been expected to share in family responsibility from the time they were very small children.

In poor families girls of 11 and 12 often went out to work. Mary Gaetano washed dishes in a boarding house; Eva Dizenfeld stripped tobacco in a cigar factory; and Margaret Kuzma delivered meat orders from the family's butcher shop each morning before school. Many young girls helped raise younger brothers and sisters and took care of housekeeping duties. Interrelated patterns of outside work and family responsibility started in childhood and continued through adult life. Historically and today, women worked and continue to work because they have to. The money they earn is an important part of their family's well-being.

For Martha Stuka, buying her son Nicky the bicycle he wanted motivated her to seek her first job. Fannie Robbins opened her own business when her husband suffered a nervous breakdown. Jane Gaida worked nights cleaning office buildings to support her aged parents. Mildred Reich sold lingerie in a department store to pay for her son's education.

Milka Vojnic worked on the railroad. I am going to repeat Mrs. Vojnic's story in her own words because I believe her experience and the feelings she expressed can be an inspiration to all of us. She said:

"From the time she was in kindergarten my daughter Anna wanted to go to college . . . When she finished high school she worked in the library for 50 cents an hour, and she cried to me, 'Mom, at this rate it will take me twenty years to save for college!'

"Well, it was wartime; women were needed to do heavy labor, and I got a job on the railroad. I had to carry hundred-pound sacks of ice in the dining cars and big full garbage cans down from the train. It was freezing; there were icicles on my pants.

"I didn't bring my pay home. Instead, I put every penny in the Building and Loan Society, because I knew that if I brought it home we would spend it to live. I saved until I could say to Anna, 'Now you can go to college.'"

As I left Mrs. Vojnic's house I asked her, "Was there anything you did in your life that made you feel very good?" She answered rather shyly, trying not to sound immodest, "When I was working on the railroad I loved my job. I worked hard, like a man. Two hundred pounds of ice I carried at once and I chopped it in the diner, but I was never tired when I came home. I was more than satisfied to put that money away for my daughter's college. That's what made me more satisfied and more happy than anything."

Mrs. Vojnic's story is one example of the close historic connection between work, family, and self-esteem.

She and the other women mentioned above were well past 70 when they recalled their work experience. However, the connection between work and family persisted just as strongly among their daughters. Whether they worked as part-time secretaries or pursued professional careers, women spoke of the central importance of family in their lives.

Dr. Wanda Nied, a physician in private practice since 1949, decided when her daughter was born that she would be the best mother in the world as well as the best doctor. Although her own mother came to babysit, Dr. Nied did not want her to bathe the baby, insisting, "That's my responsibility." (Not many husbands shared in child-care in those days.)

At the age of 53 Dr. Nied carried on a busy medical practice and at the same time supervised the care of her mother, who was then an invalid and lived in an apartment above the office. Dr. Nied spent evenings at her suburban home with her husband, cooking, talking, and cleaning the house. Two grandchildren came to spend each weekend with the Nieds so that their parents could enjoy some free time. Dr. Nied gave of her boundless energy equally to work and family, bringing happiness to others and finding satisfaction herself. She seems to have been able to "do it all."

Sometimes younger women feel a great deal of stress when they try to combine work and family. There are many reasons: Grandparents live far away; work takes place far from home; child-care presents a problem; and husbands often object. Ruthie Harter, a social worker and mother of a year-old baby, spoke of her feelings of conflict between work and family. "I want a balanced life," she said. "Can you suggest a way that a woman can pursue a career and not have to give up the family half of herself?"

Needs, Success, and Family

Many women are concerned with this issue, for all human beings have a basic need to experience personal achievement. Work is one creative path to achievement.

A famous psychologist, Abraham Maslow, developed the theory of a pyramid of human needs common to all people. At the top of the pyramid is the point of self-actualization, the highest aspiration a human being can have. Very few of us reach this stage, because all of our lower needs must be met first. Basic survival needs for food, drink, and safety must be satisfied. Then we must fill our social need to belong and to feel love and approval. (For most of us, family plays the central role in filling our social need.) Near the top of the pyramid is achievement, the source of self-esteem that comes through work. Self-actualization can be reached only after the first four needs are fulfilled and integrated.

One remark I have heard in many variations in my conversations with women is, "I would love to do something on my own, but my family thinks it will be too much for me." The discouragement of husbands or parents or children has long held many women back from individual achievement. And this is perfectly understandable. According to Maslow, it is humanly impossible to aspire to self-accomplishment if we lose all love and approval. And it is painful to lose even a little bit when family is of central value in our lives.

In my search for an integrated life I am reminded

often of the importance of the people I love. I need my family's support in order to give 100 percent enthusiasm to my work. *Women cannot and should not have to sacrifice approval and love for the sake of personal achievement.* Yet, do you know that lack of family support causes many women to avoid accomplishment and to express a fear of success?

Men do not encounter this conflict when they seek achievement in their careers. They feel more free to channel their energies toward getting ahead, toward recognition, promotion, and greater income. As a man moves up in the world he receives increasing support from his family, his colleagues, and his friends.

The story is quite different for women. Instead of love and approval, women are often punished for achievement by isolation and criticism. Husbands frequently resist the idea of wives going to work. A recent Gallup Poll reported that more than one-third of American women considered an ideal life to include marriage, children, and a full-time job. Twenty-nine percent of the full-time homemakers between the ages of 35 and 49 said they stayed at home because their husbands did not want them to work.

How to deal with a husband who opposes the idea of a working wife? In order to turn that resistance into support, it is important to understand why the husband objects; what it is that he may fear. First of all, love and caring may explain in part his reluctance to see his wife enter the world of work. Husbands value the intimate relationship of marriage and want a wife who is also a companion. A husband may be afraid that his wife's commitment to a job will reduce the time and attention that she now devotes to him.

Secondly, a husband may feel that a working wife will neglect the house and the children. He may be wondering, "Will she cook dinner or will she want to go out?" Or "What if Tommy or Barby gets sick?" Or "What extra responsibilities will this mean for me?"

Third, traditional stereotypes continue to affect attitudes. Many husbands are uncomfortable with the idea of a working wife because they were brought up to believe that the man should be the breadwinner and the woman should be the full-time mother/homemaker. Historically women worked in order to supplement the family's income, and the ability to support a wife at home signaled the husband's success.

I remember that when we were first married my husband said "No wife of mine will ever work!" Years later, when I understood the reasons behind his feelings, it was natural and easy to change his mind.

Here are three effective methods for a wife to use in changing resistance to cooperation and opposition to support. First of all, assure your family that your need to work in no way lessens your love and caring for each of them. All of us can demonstrate commitment to our loved ones by giving ourselves fully in the time we have together, devoting our full attention to them, and relaxing and letting go in play and social activities.

As a second and most important step, *share your goals* with the people whose opinions you value. When I began my research I discussed the work with my husband, my children, and my mother, letting all of them know how important my work was to me and how much I valued their support. And this made all the difference. Once my family understood, they accepted the reality of my needs.

This experience teaches that we cannot expect anyone, even people we love, to read our minds. We must *express* our wants and needs in order to enlist the support necessary to achieve them. And involving your loved ones in your work integrates family and achievement goals in a positive way.

A third step you can take to effectively increase your family's cooperation is to give to the people you love the kind of support you expect them to give to you.

Motivation and the Family Connection

Motivation is what gets us going and keeps us trying. Motivation brings success. One of the most effective motivators is family responsibility. Historically employers have always preferred to hire married men rather than single men. They believed that a man with family responsibility would try harder and do a better job. Yet, when women look for jobs business often takes the opposite view. A personnel director may remark, "We can't count on you; you'll be too busy with your family."

Actually, having a family is often a strong motivator for a woman. For all of us, women as well as men, parenthood often acts as the catalyst for career achievement. Do you know a woman who was "just working" until she became a parent? Was she then inspired to achieve, perform creatively, and become financially successful? This happened to me when my third child was born. Suddenly I realized that we had a big family. While I had held jobs before, I now began to think in terms of my *career*.

Setting Goals and Organizing Time

"All right," you may say as you read this, "I'm motivated—but *how can I fit it all in?* The day has only twenty-four hours!"

Time is a funny thing. Everybody has exactly the same amount, but we all use it differently. If you have a home or family you are already a natural expert at time management. Women have an edge here. Each day women juggle shopping, meals, work, driving, errands, doctors' visits, meetings, social life, telephone calls, and visits to parents. Somehow we manage.

My son taught me a basic management lesson that he learned as a college freshman. At the first meeting of the psychology class Norm's professor wrote on the blackboard the letters *T A N F L*. They stand for "There Ain't No Free Lunch," for to achieve one goal we pay by giving up something else.

Most of us are so busy doing what we think we have to do that we do not think about what we really want to do. The first step towards integrating our achievement and family needs is to set specific goals. When we decide exactly what is most important we will give up the distracting, time-consuming activities that accomplish little more than filling the hours.

"All this is fine," you may say, "for lucky people who know exactly what they want. But what about me? I am interested in so many different things. How can I ever decide?"

This was one of my difficulties, and I would like to share a few ideas which have helped me to focus on specific goals.

1. *Dream the impossible dream.* Picture what you would like more than anything else in the world. Write it down so that you don't forget your fantasy.

2. *Set yourself up for success.* Attempt the possible. Think about that dream of yours; focus in on it and write down what part of it you can make come true.

3. *Formulate a reachable goal.* Make it compatible with personal and family values.

4. *Share your goals with your family.* Plan with the per-

son closest to you to set aside a short time each week to talk about your progress toward your goal. The weekly report will motivate you to stick to your plan.

To Tomorrow!

The great freedom women enjoy today is a valuable gift. Yet this very freedom represents a challenge, for freedom implies responsibility. Women today have options. We choose our own lives and we are responsible for the consequences. Women like Jane Gaida and Milka Vojnic and Fannie Robbins did not plan and choose their work. They made decisions on the spur of the moment because of poverty, an unforeseen emergency, or the special needs of one family member.

Today the situation is quite different. Women decide *whether* to work and *what kind* of work they will do. A woman may decide to pursue full-time work along with family responsibility. That is your choice and your challenge and you can meet that challenge positively and affirmatively.

Women who choose to work want to be successful. But what is success? The oral history interviews suggested this definition: Success is that *feeling good* that comes with achievement, accompanied by love and approval from people we care about the most—our families.

The successful women in history and the successful women today are those who are able to integrate achievement and family goals. As family is the traditional reality, freedom of choice is the new reality. And women can learn to use both traditions—the values deep within—and their new decision-power to enrich their lives. Like the ideal woman in the Bible, we will face the future with a smile.

Dr. H. PAUL JACOBI

Dr. Jacobi received his degree from Marquette University in 1950. He is a fellow of the Academy of General Dentistry, president-elect and board member of the Canadian-American Medical Dental Association, and a member of the American Academy of Dental Practice Administration. He has served as president of the Neenah-Menasha Dental Society, Winnebago County Dental Society, and Fox River Valley Dental Society in Wisconsin. He is a past president of the Neenah Lions Club, past exalted ruler of the Neenah-Menasha Elks Lodge, a member of the Neenah Rotary Club, SME (Sales and Marketing Executives International), and the National Speakers Association.

He has addressed audiences throughout the world

and in most major cities of the United States and lectured on a post-graduate level at many universities including Marquette, Louisiana State, Fairleigh Dickinson, Medical University of South Carolina, Case Western, and Georgetown. He has been a featured speaker for the International Society of Advanced Education and the Albert Einstein Institute.

Dr. Jacobi is the author of *A Dentist's Flight Manual to Success,* the cassette series "A Dentist's Flight to Success," and the booklet "Dental DAFFYnitions"; a co-author of *Consumers Dental Bible;* and creator of the Personal Dental Record Forms. He has served as guest editorialist for *Dental Survey Magazine;* as guest writer for *Dental Management, Oral Health,* and *Dental Economics* magazines; and as a contributing writer for *The Dental Practitioner,* a newspaper for the New Zealand dentist.

He is a member of the executive committee of the Organization of Teachers of Dental Practice Administration; vice president of Professionals of America Corporation, Scottsdale, Arizona; and president of Project P, Inc., Neenah, Wisconsin. In addition he serves as professional management consultant to Professional Service Corporation, Inc., Madison, Wisconsin.

Dr. Jacobi was selected for *Who's Who in the Midwest* in the 1978, 1979, 1980, and 1981 editions. He serves as an advisor to the Wisconsin State Dentistry Examining Board and maintains an active practice in Neenah.

You can contact Dr. Jacobi by writing to him at Project P, Inc., 448 Edgewood Court, Neenah, WI 54956; or telephone (414) 725-5668.

TO BE OR NOT TO BE...
DIFFERENT

by Dr. H. PAUL JACOBI

People are not created equal. That's a popular, time-honored myth. We're all created different. Our parents, our heritage, our environment, and our social, religious, and economic backgrounds differ. And our intellects differ. Newborn babies have their own unique personalities. (Ask any nurse in a maternity ward.) We're born different and we grow up to be different.

Have you ever heard the story about the little pip-squeaky guy who wanted a job as a lumberjack?

The foreman of the lumber camp told him, "We're looking for *men* around here!"

The little guy said, "I can cut wood. I can chop down trees."

So the foreman gave him an hour to see what he

could chop down in the back forty.

After only 45 minutes the little guy was back, asking "What do you want me to do now?"

"Why did you stop?" asked the foreman. "I told you to cut for an hour. Is 45 minutes as long as you can work?"

"Oh, no," replied the little guy. "I'm all done. I cut 'em all down."

The foreman went to see for himself and, sure enough, the back forty was leveled.

"Where'd you ever learn to cut wood like that?" he asked incredulously.

"In the Sahara Forest," the little guy told him.

"You mean the Sahara Desert?"

"Well *now*," said the little guy.

To be or not to be . . . different. What do you choose for your life? That question is the message I offer you.

The Uncommon Man

Equality, conformity, mediocrity—that is the philosophy of failure. Anyone can float down the river of mediocrity. It's not very deep, it's not very challenging, and it's filled with negative thinkers floating downstream like dead fish. (Live fish swim upstream seeking challenge and opportunity. It's the same with live people.)

Sometimes the only thing that stands between you and your life goal is the will to try and the faith to be different. Most everyone will tell you you can't be different. It's easy to find someone to say you can't achieve your goal. The person who's never made $20,000 a year knows all the reasons why you can't make $25,000. But if you have a dream, no matter what it is, dare to *believe* in it and try to make it come true. Be *different*, not equal. There's never yet been a statue erected to the memory of someone who let well enough alone.

Do you want to become a leader? Leadership involves paying a price. For one thing, a leader never knows whether he is being followed or chased. A leader leads by example. That's the real difference between a boss and a leader. A boss tells you what to do and a leader *shows you how to do it.*

Everyone knows that people will work for money. They will work harder for a leader. But the best motivator is something in which they believe. Why not believe in the challenge of excellence, the knock of opportunity, and the pursuit of happiness? Become contagiously enthusiastic about yourself and your work.

People who succeed in life display contagious enthusiasm. They possess self-confidence. They build on their strengths and ignore their weaknesses. They maintain a positive mental attitude, concentrating on their ability to succeed. A positive mental attitude involves expectation and purpose. But above all, it involves setting worthy goals that are desirable and attainable.

Successful people set goals in which they can believe. When they achieve their high goals, others may call them lucky. But luck is overrated and misunderstood. It is the *prepared person who is looking for an opportunity* who will be able to grasp it when it comes along. The true basis of "luck" is having a plan to succeed.

You've surely heard the words "The harder I work, the luckier I get," but I'll bet you've never heard them from a loser. Show me a good loser and I'll show you a loser without a plan to succeed! Just as success needs no excuse, poverty needs no plan.

In an age where "doing your own thing" is so prized, discipline is often overlooked. I believe that self-discipline is essential for being different. Self-discipline of mind and body is the catalyst required for fulfilling your own potential.

We are continually tempted to leave our intended paths. So often we succumb. Consider all the possible pitfalls strewn along the career path of a college student: Why not go out for a beer with the gang instead of studying an hour longer? Use crib notes instead of preparing thoroughly? Take a less arduous load and have a little goof-off time?

It's always tempting to take the easier road. Self-discipline involves *doing the thing you'd rather not do.* (A valuable trick is to always do the thing you don't want to do first. Put it at the top of your list and get it over with.)

This principle was epitomized by Notre Dame's famous football coach, Knute Rockne. He was the one who said, "When the going gets tough, the tough get going."

The gap between what a person thinks he can achieve and what he actually can achieve varies within each of us. But as Napoleon Hill said, "What the mind can conceive and believe *it can achieve.*" Those are not empty words.

Let me ask you a thought-provoking question: Who is it who stands in the way of your distinguishing yourself?

And another question: Who's Number One in your book? Some people will answer God, wife, husband, girlfriend, mother, son, or daughter. What is your answer? Have you considered that *you* may be Number One? If you don't prize yourself, who will? If you don't think well of yourself, why would anybody else?

Unfortunately, well-intentioned people often transmit negative signals and stimulate negative thoughts. The frequency of these signals and the tone of these thoughts can contribute to a negative attitude. They help to form the basis of our feelings toward the world around us, with either positive or negative reinforcements.

The negative person sees difficulty in every opportunity and the positive person sees opportunity in every difficulty. There's an undocumented story about a large aircraft manufacturer that wanted a government contract for a new supersonic airplane. They had all the engineers working and all the great planners working, but every time the plane got up to the speed of sound, the wings fell off. The company really wanted that contract, so they offered a $10,000 award for a solution to the problem.

Suggestion after suggestion failed. Finally, there was an unsigned crumpled piece of paper in the suggestion box. It said, "Poke little holes between the wing and the fuselage."

The company president said, "This has got to be nuts, but we'll try it." It worked, and they got the contract.

For two years they tried to find out who came up with the saving idea. Then one evening when the president was working late, the janitor came into his office and asked, "Hey boss, did you ever use my suggestion to put those holes between the wings and the fuselage?"

The president was surprised that the janitor knew anything about aerodynamic design. He asked him about his background.

The janitor replied, "I don't know anything about aerodynamic design. But I've been a janitor here for 20 years and there's one thing I do know. Toilet paper never tears where the holes are."

Unfortunately, people have been groomed to think negatively about positive thoughts and positively about negative thoughts. Dr. Robert Schuller once said that God's easiest task is to make us humble, and His most difficult task is to make us positive.

When I speak to dental groups, I liken the dental office to an airplane. The dentist is the pilot, his staff is the crew, and the patients are the passengers. I remind them that the biggest airplane in the world can't back up by itself; a 747 is designed to go forward. No airplane was designed to taxi down the runway, either. They all were designed to fly high in the sky, above the clouds, above the storms.

Then I make a comparison with people. How many people do you know who spend their lives taxiing down the runway of life, revving their engines, but afraid to take off? *We were all designed to fly!* But so often we don't want to lose the security of keeping one foot on the ground. We haven't got the guts to get out of ruts.

In a commencement speech at Harvard, Russian exile Alexander Solzhenitsyn said, "A loss of courage may be the most striking feature which an outside observer notices in the West in our day." Should one point out that from ancient times, decline in courage is considered to be the beginning of the end?

Sometimes it takes uncommon courage to rise above the crowd. It takes the true courage of conviction to stand up and be counted for what we believe to be right, instead of letting others do our thinking for us.

Why not be different? Why not think differently? That's how new ideas are created and fortunes made. Why not lead the field with constructive thinking based on facts instead of on fads or prejudice or political affiliation?

When we accept other people's thinking, it's so easy to jump to the wrong conclusion.

(That reminds me of the little city boy who saw a fat pig out at the farm. When the farmer asked him if he knew why the pig was so fat, he said, "Sure, I just saw six little piggies blowing her up.")

Let's face it. The one unique quality we each have

going for us is not that we're equal, but that we're different.

Some of us are loaded with positive mental attitude, PMA. (You can also spell it GAS—goals, ambition, and success.) Some of us are square—square with the world, given a square deal, and can look a person square in the eye. And some of us are round—rolling down any hill that comes along so long as we get pushed or shoved into the path of least resistance. Some of us shed responsibilities and problems like water, and some of us are of definite purpose and stand up for what we believe is right.

Here's a real success story with a twist. A few years ago one of the most famous restaurants on the Boston waterfront held an opening night celebration. It was a special party held for some very special guests, and it was spectacular. To this day, if you ask a cabby for the name of a good waterfront restaurant in Boston he'll reply, "Let me take you to Anthony's, Pier Four." Why? Because the honored guests for that opening night extravaganza were the cabbies of Boston and their spouses.

Sometimes being different is a question of creative alternatives. If you've ever been to San Diego, you've probably marveled at the sights. One particular landmark has a very interesting history. Near the turn of the century there was need for a new elevator inside the El Cortez Hotel. Construction of the elevator would destroy choice rooms and create a shambles, with dust, dirt, and debris everywhere. A distraught janitor suggested, "Why don't you build that thing on the *outside* of the building?" Nobody had thought of that. The same idea was put to use at the Fairmont in San Francisco. An uncommon man had an uncommon vision.

The common man dogma needs some revision. This may be the era of the common man, but it is the *uncommon man* who takes the calculated risk and achieves the reward. Isn't it the *uncommon* educator we really want for our sons and daughters? Isn't it the *uncommon* general we want to lead us in battle? Is it the average President we want or need or is it the *uncommon* one? And I ask you, if your kids were sick, really sick, would you prefer the common doctor or the *uncommon* one?

Mediocrity is like hitching your life to a cloud instead of a star. Clouds obstruct light and warmth, create worries and doubts, postpone dreams and aspirations. When you are hitched to a cloud, you move with the wind whichever way it blows.

One way to overcome mediocrity is to picture the person you most admire. List that person's outstanding qualities. Now picture the person you admire the least. Write down the qualities you associate with him. Have you learned something?

Mediocrity can best be defined as the place in the middle, the best of the worst and the worst of the best. But who wants to live in a place like that? It's easier to go down the hill than up, but isn't the view much better at the top?

There's no sense waiting for our ship to come in if we haven't sent one out. In his book *As a Man Thinketh*, James Allen wrote: "Whatever your present environment may be, you will fall, remain, or rise with your thoughts, your visions, your ideals. You will become as small as your controlling desire or as great as your dominant aspiration."

Winning Ways

I have found that successful people have ten distinguishing characteristics and I would like to share them with you.

1. *They have a contagious enthusiasm.* They're fun to be with; they've got charisma.

2. *They radiate self-confidence.* They believe in themselves; they have the courage of their convictions.

3. *They've got PMA—Positive Mental Attitude.* They "accentuate the positive, eliminate the negative, and don't mess with Mr. In-Between."

4. *They're goal strivers.* They're filled with GAS— Goals, Ambition, Success. They're persistent achievers. They've an insatiable appetite to stay on top. They're action people. They carry on in spite of opposition or failure. They recognize that every failure brings with it the seed of an equivalent advantage.

5. *They focus on their strengths.* They know they can't be the best in everything they do. They strive for excellence, not perfection. They know that one of the most frustrating things in the world is to set goals so high that there's no way to achieve them.

6. *They smile a lot.* They wear a happy face, but they aren't afraid to take it off with at least one person they love.

7. *They're generous.* They willingly share their time and their talent. Truly successful people won't shoot you down. They're happy to go the extra, undemanded mile to help you.

8. *They've got mental toughness.* They have the self-discipline that results in the achievement of a worthy goal. It's characterized by an invigorating determination to achieve their goals on time and on target.

9. *They're good at role-playing.* They can change gears, wear a different hat, and do it effectively. They can switch the pitch or hit the ditch. (No successful per-

son can apply identical methods at home as in the office.)

10. *They're humble and gentle in success.* They are not aloof or pretentious. Their strengths lie in their gentleness. They don't come on as being superior, while making you feel inferior.

I'm reminded of the story of the Texan who was driving through Louisiana in his big Mercedes. He saw a small chicken farm along the road and he asked the farmer "Hey, friend! How far down does your property line go?"

The chicken farmer told him "Oh, about a hundred feet."

The big Texan reared back and laughed. "On my ranch," he said, "I take my big pickup truck and I go down my property line in the morning, and it's the middle of the afternoon before I finally get back to my ranch house."

The chicken farmer replied, "Yeah, I had a pickup like that once too."

No one can make you feel inferior without your consent. They can only stimulate the feeling that is already there, waiting to be poked at.

What do you want to be? If you want to be a happy, positive, enthusiastic person, stay with happy, positive, enthusiastic people. If you want to learn about success, stay with successful people. If you want to catch the flu, stay with fellows who have it. It's all contagious. And confidence breeds confidence.

The Possible Dream

Write down your long-range goals. They will keep you from becoming frustrated by short-term failure. One of the fine points of becoming goal-oriented is to be able to distinguish between goals and tasks. Merely going to work in the morning and spending all day working will accomplish the task of working; but it has nothing to do with goals. You can spend a lifetime working, but unless you have something you are working *toward*—a realistic, believable, desirable, and attainable goal—you merely go through the motions of work without feeling achievement. It's as frustrating as shooting a gun without aiming at a target.

Task orientation provides no rewards. Why not switch the pitch right now and *set goals?* Get out on the limb, because that's where the fruit is.

You know, you really don't pay a price for success, you pay a price to get there. Once you're there, then you enjoy it. *But you do pay a price for failure.*

A friend remarked the other day that our advanced technology has developed a $15,000 car which will rust out after five years and a beer can which when discarded will last forever.

I'm sure that you know people who have rusted out in a few years. I have. But I've seen very few winners rust out. (I've seen a few burn out, though, from taking themselves too seriously.)

It's been said that the age of a man is determined by the amount of pain he experiences when he hears a new idea. In 1976, when we celebrated our country's 200th birthday, I was about to celebrate my 50th. I figured that made me one-fourth as old as our country. I also figured out that in 25 years I would be 75 and our country would be 225. Then I would be one-third as old as our country. Then I figured that when I was 150, our country would be 300 years old and I'd only be half as old as our country. At that rate, before too long I'd catch up all the way. That's what I call positive mental attitude!

I would like to share with you the creed of attorney Dean Alfange:

I do not choose to be a common man. It's my right to be uncommon if I can. I seek opportunity, not security. I do not wish to be a kept citizen, humbled and dulled by having the state look after me. I want to take the calculated risk to dream and to build, to fail and to succeed. I refuse to barter incentive for a dole. I prefer the challenges of life to the guaranteed existence, the thrill of fulfillment to the calm of utopia. I will not trade freedom for beneficence nor dignity for a hand-out. It's my heritage to stand erect, unbending and unafraid—to enjoy the benefits of my creations, face the world boldly, and say, 'This I have done. This is what it means to me to be an American.'

DOROTHY
JONGEWARD, Ph.D.

Dorothy Jongeward, co-author of the two-million-copy bestseller *Born to Win*, is an internationally known consultant in personal and organizational effectiveness. She is a prominent lecturer, author, and educator who pioneers in the application of transactional analysis to people-problems within organizations.

Dr. Jongeward consults for business, industry, educational institutions, and government. She lectures and conducts workshops for a wide variety of groups and has made presentations in Montreal, London, Johannesburg, Cape Town, Brisbane, Sydney, Melbourne, Hamburg, Milan, and Oslo.

She works extensively in the area of understanding the unique problems of contemporary women. She testified on behalf of women's education at the California Advisory Commission on the Status of Women in May 1966 and designed a three-day seminar for women in government which has become an affirmative action model for women's programs.

Dr. Jongeward is president of the Transactional Analysis Management Institute, Inc., and a professor of human behavior and transactional analysis at California American University. She is a state-licensed marriage, family, and child counselor and a life member of the California Association of Marriage and Family Counselors.

Dr. Jongeward is listed in *Contemporary Authors, Who's Who in Religion, The World Who's Who of Women,* and *Men and Women of Distinction.*

In addition to *Born to Win,* Dr. Jongeward has written numerous articles for professional publications. She has authored or co-authored the following books: *Choosing Success: Transactional Analysis on the Job; Women as Winners: Transactional Analysis for Personal Growth; Winning with People: Group Exercises in Transactional Analysis; Affirmative Action for Women: A Practical Guide for Women and Management; The People Book: Transactional Analysis for Students;* and *Winning Ways in Health Care: Transactional Analysis for Effective Communication.*

This chapter is an edited excerpt from chapters two and three in her book *Everybody Wins: Transactional Analysis Applied to Organizations,* Addison-Wesley Publishing Company, 1973. *Everybody Wins* was selected by the *Library Journal* as one of the ten best business books in 1974.

You may contact Dorothy Jongeward by writing to Transactional Analysis Management Institute, Inc., 724 Ironbark Court, Orinda, CA 94563. Telephone (415) 254-4117.

STOP PLAYING THOSE GAMES!

by DOROTHY JONGEWARD, Ph.D.

A social worker retorts, "Well, I was only trying to help you!"

A staff person blames, "If it weren't for the old man upstairs, we'd have this project well on its way."

A stewardess complains, "I don't see why all the weird things always happen to me."

A company lawyer gleams, "This is the fourth time he's botched up a job for us. We've got him cold this time."

Psychological games can be a powerful force in preventing people from becoming winners.

Every game has a hidden agenda. People playing games are not really talking about what it sounds as if they're talking about. The hidden motive discounts the players. Someone collects negative strokes. Someone gets hurt. Real problems go unsolved.

Games played by employees are costly in terms of their own success and the success of the organization they work for. People who otherwise could be productive divert their psychic and physical energies into their games rather than into getting the job done, making the decision, or solving the problem. Awareness focuses on past events rather than the current reality of the work scene. If the reality of a situation goes unperceived, problems go unsolved.

Games played in organizations are not necessarily different from games played at home. People play games wherever they are with people. This chapter, however, deals with what motivates game-playing on the job, illustrates extensively how certain games are acted out in the organizational setting, and demonstrates how some games can be broken up.

WHY PEOPLE PLAY GAMES

Most of what occurs in a game is destructive, at least to some degree. Naturally, the intensity with which people play games varies. Some games gain social approval. Some are played for keeps and end up in prison or the morgue.

Games are a way to fill up time. Structuring time is a basic human need. If time is not structured, people suffer boredom. Boredom encourages physical and mental deterioration. *People bored with their jobs are more prone to game-playing.*

The need for strokes (any act of touch or recognition) is also universal. We all need strokes to survive and negative strokes are better than none. People get strokes from playing games, even though these strokes are negative.

For example, a person who plays a game of *Stupid* does stupid things and collects put-downs. Each time the game is played, the player reinforces a negative stroke pattern learned in childhood, adding to a collection of "stupid" psychological trading stamps. *If the work environment is void of positive strokes, people have more need to play games.*

Games reinforce our psychological positions. Games always strengthen a sense of I'm not-OK and/or You're not-OK. People who take the position "I'm stupid," begin to act stupid. In this sense, such people are stuck maintaining their own status quos. *Company time can be used to reinforce old negative self/other concepts.*

Games assist in avoiding or regulating intimacy. While people engage in games, they avoid authentic, honest, or open encounter. Some organizations discourage openness and honesty. *Authenticity on the job can be foiled by game-playing.*

Organizations may foster certain games. For example, a hierarchy structure encourages games like *If It Weren't for Him (Them)*. Individuals or groups within an organization who play this game blame someone else either above or below them for their problems. It is a way to pass the buck. Players of such games render themselves pure and blameless by placing the responsibility on someone else. *See What You Made Me Do* is another blaming game. People play this one to blame their mistakes on someone either up or down the ladder.

In some organizations, in order for employees to follow the upward mobility patterns they must develop a strong sense of competition and undercutting rather than teamwork and cooperativeness. In such cases, in addition to the blaming games, games that catch people up or point out their mistakes are likely to be prevalent. *Now I've Got You—You S.O.B., Blemish,* and *Bear Trapper* help to fulfill these organizational dictates. In *Now I've Got You* someone ends up being caught for having made a mistake. In *Blemish*, tiny, inconsequential mistakes are pointed out. In *Bear Trapper* the trap falls on an employee who may then have to decide whether to stick with the organization or to seek employment elsewhere.

Some organizations, rather than stroking cooperativeness, stroke and expect employees to play the undercutting games. In addition to those games mentioned, organizations may encourage the one-upmanship style games. Employees may feel compelled to act these out in order to "get ahead." This climate encourages *Let's You and Him Fight* and variations of the game *Mine's Better than Yours*, such as *I'm Closer to the Boss Than You*. These games need to be only slightly adapted as a person moves up through the hierarchy structure.

COMMON PSYCHOLOGICAL GAMES

This section illustrates how some individual games are adapted to the work setting. As you read through the following games, be aware of the time each structures, the kind of strokes involved, the avoidance of decision-making or problem-solving, and the investment of time and energy in the past rather than the present.

Yes, But

The game of *Why Don't You? – Yes, But* is very likely one of the most common played between staff and line individuals. It's a way to put people down, quite frequently without their being fully aware of it. There is a special payoff if the game puts down the "experts" or anyone else, such as a consultant, who takes a helpful or authoritative stance. *Yes, But* players only *appear* to be looking for helpful solutions to problems. In the end, any advice they receive is rejected. As a consequence, the person the game is played with ends up being defined as not-OK.

Almost everyone at some time or other has experienced a *Yes, But* game. In *Yes, But* the person who is "it" (the initiator of the game) lays out a problem. The problem is the hook. The others give advice or possible solutions to a problem.

On the plausible Adult-to-Adult level the transaction appears to be, "I have this problem and I would like you to help me solve it." The response on the plausible Adult-to-Adult level might be, "Yes, I have some good ideas to help you solve your problem and here they are."

At the ulterior level the Child in the initiator of the game is actually saying, "I have this problem. You just *try* to help me solve it and I'll put you down!" If hooked, the responder may continue to give solutions for a long time in the effort to "help" the other person, who has an inexhaustible list of reasons why the solutions won't work.

Yes, But players often structure time in a business meeting to play their game.

Problems that need genuine solutions go unsolved. The energies are invested in playing the game (for the payoff of rejecting the advice and ideas of others) rather than in the solution of the problem.

Yes, But is not always played in meetings; it can be played in a hallway when one person stops the other with, "Say, you know there is something that is really bothering me," and then states the problem. The other person may be hooked into this interaction for 40 minutes and go away with the feeling of, "Good grief—no matter what I say to that guy, it's not going to work."

Learning not to be hooked into a *Yes, But* game can save a great amount of time. The classical solution is to refuse to offer advice or answers. If a player starts a game,

"I'm having the worst time trying to get those clerks mo- tivated to take more training," a responder may withhold suggestions with, "That can be rough, Mabel. What are your plans?"

See What You Made Me Do

This is a common blaming game. The person who plays this game makes a mistake in the presence of another person and then blames that mistake on the other person. For example, a lab worker concentrates on a slide as the supervisor approaches. Just as the supervisor looks over his shoulder, the lab worker drops the slide and turns an- grily to his supervisor, saying, "See what you made me do!"

Once I was giving a workshop in an industrial setting and had just finished explaining this game. At that very moment a loud crash was heard in the hallway. Someone had dropped a tray of test tubes that went crashing, scat- tering down the hallway. In the midst of the noise and hubbub, a man hollered out, "See what you made me do!" I'm sure the workshop participants thought I had set this one up.

Another common version of the game is the typist who makes an error when the supervisor walks by, and then, instead of taking the responsibility for the mistake, turns angrily to the supervisor, saying "See what you made me do!"

The individual who plays *See What You Made Me Do* is often a collector of angry feelings about others and in- adequacy feelings about self. Sometimes, however, this person is collecting feelings of self-righteousness and pu- rity: "Nothing is ever my fault, but it's yours." This is similar to the disclaimer for not-OK behavior, "The devil made me do it."

If It Weren't for You

This is another blaming game. People who play it often feel inadequate themselves and cop out on their own achievement or development, blaming their inability to achieve on others. In one company this game went something like this:

For two years T.C. complained that if it weren't for D.J., he would have long since been the manager of the department. In T.C.'s eyes, D.J. was unfair, uncommunicative, and seemed to take a special pleasure in holding people back. D.J. was then unexpectedly transferred to another plant in another state. The head of the department went to T.C. with the good news, "D.J.'s job is now yours. You've wanted this promotion for a long time." To the manager's surprise, T.C. became frustrated rather than joyful, and he eventually quit.

In the above case, T.C. had gotten satisfaction out of blaming someone else for the lack of promotions. When the chips were down and he was offered the job, he backed off.

In a similar situation, a woman manager complained that if it weren't for the size of her office, the productivity in her division would be higher. When the plant was eventually expanded, her working area was given special attention, and it was considerably enlarged. After six weeks of working in the new surroundings, this manager asked for a transfer to another division. It was known that the division which she asked for was housed in very small quarters in another part of the state.

This game often baffles people in personnel. Someone complains "If It Weren't for Something or Someone," yet when they get their chance, they don't come through.

It is useful to watch for the words "If it weren't for . . ." as a clue to the possibility of a game involvement rather than an honest complaint.

41

Let's You and Him Fight

This game involves at least three hands. One person goes to a second person in an attempt to engage the second and third person in an argument. It is not uncommon for a game to start as *Let's You and Him Fight* between W.J. and M.H. and end up as *Uproar* between M.H. and T.L. One worker, W.J., goes to another, M.H., saying in confidence, "It makes me feel terrible to tell you this, but I thought it over and think you need to know what T.L. is saying about you." And then the person proceeds to reveal, distort, or fabricate what T.L. is saying. It is likely that M.H. will soon engage in a conflict with T.L.

Blemish

The *Blemish* player is the office nitpicker. The person who plays *Blemish* is looking for the little flaw or the Achilles' heel. A *Blemish* player may read through a ten-page report and call attention only to a comma or a semicolon or a word that is misspelled. This kind of game-player tends to pay far more attention to tiny, inconsequential details than to full content.

An instructor playing *Blemish* while reading over a student's work is likely to whip out the red pencil and mark only those mistakes that don't make any difference anyway.

Blemish players seldom write comments such as, "This is really clear," "You said this well," or "This paragraph could be understood by anyone." Instead they tend not to see the whole picture or purpose of a project, but pick on only those items that are trivial mistakes. *Blemish* players occupy themselves with minutiae.

One style of *Blemish* player almost gives a positive stroke but whips out a discount in the end. This was the style of a decorator who frequently said to a staff member something like, "That's beautiful the way you've arranged the colors. But don't you think an olive green would be better than the green you chose?"

Corner

A *Corner* player is likely to maneuver other people into a situation in which, no matter what they do, they never come out right. In one such situation worker G.S. complained, "If B.U. would just take more responsibility and be more aggressive about getting this data in on time, our whole department would run more smoothly."

When B.U. attempted to get data in on time, G.S. always found something wrong with it. B.U. had not been able to analyze clearly what had been going wrong. He expressed to me, "No matter what I do I always come up wrong. If I am not aggressive about gathering the information and having my data in, then I'm wrong. If I forge ahead, then I've reported it in a wrong way or inaccurately by his standards. It seems as if literally no matter what I do, I can't please him. There is no way to do it right. I feel like I'm damned if I do it and damned if I don't do it."

This particular feeling is typical of the individual who feels cornered. B.U. solved this particular problem by going to G.S. and asking him who he would trust to check out information. B.U. was given the name of a very competent woman who worked in this same division. The next time there was a deadline for the data sheet, B.U. met this deadline, had the data checked to see that it could not be contested, and presented it to G.S. At least with B.U., G.S.'s game was called. He no longer put B.U. in this situation of either not getting his reports done on time or not having them complete enough.

An organizational game of *Corner* that fits into many

organizational scripts regarding sex-role expectations is sometimes played with women. Aggression is described as a necessary quality for a good manager. Yet, the word *aggression* when applied to women is a negative. In such a case, a woman is in the position of being "damned" if she's aggressive and unacceptable for upward advancement if she's not.

Uproar

Uproar is another common organizational game which fits into a hierarchy structure. *Uproar* usually starts with a discount, such as a critical remark. One person may stomp into the office of another, throw a report on the desk, and accuse angrily, "You've been in this division for four years and you haven't learned to write a decent report yet."

The expectation for the complementary hand is defense: "Well, I'm sorry. I thought I had included everything that you wanted."

"What do you mean you put into this everything I wanted? You ought to know better than . . ."

This attack/defense dialogue might continue for several minutes until finally the defendant is worn out. The two people are likely to stomp away from each other in a physically angry posture.

Uproar is often a loud, shouting kind of game. However, it can also be played with a more subtle barb. Instead of an outright attack, the dialogue could have begun, "Now, this is a great improvement over your last report. However, it is still not good enough to convince top management."

The interaction may even be carried on with facial smiles and with an "I'm only trying to help you" attitude. But the dynamics continue attack/defense, attack/defense until the defendant is worn out and the people move away from each other frustrated and angry. In the last case the player uses *Yes, But* as one method of attack.

Some people counterattack and switch the hands in the game. A male supervisor called a woman in and confronted her with, "You've been spending too much time in the ladies' restroom."

Instead of the expected self-defense, the woman retorted, "Do you mean you spy on women in the restroom?"

At this unexpected counterattack, the supervisor blurted out a defensive response and the game was switched.

Poor Me

Many games are variations of *Poor Me*. The undercurrent of such games reflects positions like "I'm stupid," "I don't deserve to live," "I can't do anything right," "I'm handicapped," "I'm ugly and clumsy," "I can't help myself," "I'm no good," "I feel sorry for myself," "It's not my fault," etc. For example, *Why Does This Always Happen to Me!* and *Ain't It Awful About Me!* always reinforce some form of self-negation and self-pity.

Employees who do plenty of griping but never move to change their situation are likely to be acting out "Atlas" scripts—carrying the burdens of the world on their shoulders.

Many of the following games have some element of *Poor Me*.

Kick Me

Kick Me players say things on the job like, "I could kick myself for doing that," "That was a terrible thing for me to have done," "I've been kicking myself all day for that," or "I really felt like kicking myself." If acting out the game, the player provokes a put-down. Such players invite, manipulate, provoke others to kick them. Being fired is one of the most common forms of acting out a hard game of *Kick Me* in organizations.

Kick Me players prefer people who will kick them. Withholding the negative stroke is one way to discourage people from playing this game with you. Players will go elsewhere for their negative strokes.

In one version of this game people do indeed kick themselves. An example is the "skull game" in which people kick themselves with destructive dialogue in their own heads. "Beating myself up" is a common theme of people who were manipulated with guilt as children.

People who operate from an I'm not-OK and You're not-OK position may catch a worker in a mistake and make that person suffer. Then later, on reflection, they play a skull game of *Kick Me,* feeling great remorse: "How could I have spoken to Mr. Howell like that? I feel terrible about it." The roles switch from Persecutor to Victim.

Stupid

Stupid is a variation of *Kick Me.* The dynamics of *Stupid* are the same. There is provocation, manipulation, and/or an invitation to put the player down. However, the put-down involves putting down the person's brains or literally calling the player "stupid." *Stupid* players have learned to negate their own intelligence and to seek negative strokes from others.

One woman who played a very hard game worked as receptionist and secretary. An instance of her stupid behavior occurred when her boss came in one day, very much in a hurry, saying, "This report has to be at the home office by the day after tomorrow. I want you to give it top priority. Stop whatever you are doing and see that this gets in the mail by four o'clock."

The secretary became a little flustered but dutifully promised to put all other things aside and get this report on its way. Two weeks later there was a great deal of hubbub at the secretary's desk. She was fussing out loud about, "How could I have done this? What a stupid thing for me to do when this report was so important."

Her boss, on entering the scene, got the picture that the secretary had found the report in her desk where it had been hidden away for two weeks.

This young woman is very likely to play her game so hard that unless some therapeutic change occurs, she will be kicked off the job for being too stupid to handle the work, thus fulfilling her "loser" script compulsion.

Harried Executive

This is a common game among modern men and women, and the organization is a perfect setting in which to act it out. This is a particularly serious game. It can structure many decades of people's lives; and often, by the time the game is recognized, the players have worn out their bodies to the extent that irreparable damage has been done. Unfortunately, organizations are sometimes set up for *Harried,* and they stroke favorably this kind of behavior. One reason is that the *Harried* player comes on originally as Superman or Superwoman, able to keep all the balls in the air, able to say *yes* to all requests, and always "Johnny-on-the-spot" to take on another responsibility.

Such players structure their life's time with work—sometimes "busy work." As long as they are working hard, they maintain their false sense of "OKness." There is very little play or leisure activity or just plain inactivity in the lives of typical *Harried Executives*. If *Harrieds* try to play for relaxation, they tend to work hard at it. As *Harried* players move ahead on the job, they take on more and more work and responsibility. They are likely to bring work home at night and even on weekends. There is always one more project that can be taken on. Such a load may be carried successfully for 15 to 30 years. The player may come on competent and confident, successfully covering up an "I'm not-OK" feeling by appearing super-OK.

One woman executive discovered that by playing *Harried* she was using her work to destroy her health. She displayed a portion of her shoulder which was covered with sores that her doctor had diagnosed as "nerves."

This woman decided on the following program: complete health checkup and health plan; time out for "doing nothing"; more work delegated; saying *no* to more requests; and helping staff members to develop more independence. (*Harried Executives* often keep staff members dependent.)

At our last meeting she had made a good start on her plan. She remarked, "I've always been critical of people who are killing themselves with alcohol. I don't drink; but I've been digging my grave right here in my office."

One executive played *Harried* for 27 years, using his organization as the setting. He died falling face forward into an unfinished report that he was writing at home on a Saturday night.

No matter where or how it is acted out, the game of *Harried* is of such a serious nature that people caught up in it need to stop as soon as possible. Bringing balance into one's life means having time for oneself—time for other people, for pleasures, for resting and relaxation, as well as for work. The person stopping *Harried Executive* often has to learn how to say *no*, how to judge when an adequate day's work is done, and how to structure time in new ways—particularly in ways that will be personally fulfilling and psychically healthful.

A Phony Game of Harried

Some organizations *require* employees to play *Harried.* Unless employees look busy, overworked, and haggard, they are looked down upon somehow as not being loyal to the organization. Such a case was exposed when a man who had play-acted to the hilt to show how busy he was, how overworked he was, and how much work he took home evenings and weekends was stopped by a security officer when leaving the building. The security officer had his orders mixed up. He had been ordered to check briefcases, purses, and any bags carried into the building. But somehow on his first day, he confused the directions and was examining briefcases, etc., as people *left* the building. When this particular executive was forced to open his briefcase, it was found to be filled with *Playboy* magazines. Rather than doing homework, he had a little bag full of goodies which he fantasied with on the commuter bus.

A variation of *Phony Harried* is a game I've come to call *Don't Give It to Me to Do.* One woman caseworker stacked files on her desk until they were piled high. This gave the appearance that she had far too much to do. However, it was discovered that these were mainly completed cases. The purpose that it served for her was to avoid work, to avoid a load of things to do. People would walk up to her desk with a case file in their hands, see that she had more than she could possibly handle, and walk away without saying anything. The message that this *Harried*-appearing desk gave to other people was "Don't give it to me to do. See how much I'm doing already!"

These games are called phony because they are not motivated by a childhood decision but are a response to the work situation. Players are usually aware of what they are doing.

HOW TO SIDESTEP A GAME

Without information, most of us play our games in a completely unaware way. When a game is over, however, we often have some awareness that the "same old thing" has happened one more time.

The repetitive nature of games is one way to begin to recognize them. It is not unusual for us to find ourselves repeating almost the same series of transactions again and again, perhaps with the same person.

Games structure differing amounts of time. Games such as *Kick Me* or *Blemish* may be over in a few minutes while *Alcoholic*, *Debtor*, or *Harried* may fill up a lifetime.

Adult input about games helps us become aware of them, recognize them, and consider options. Usually the first step is hindsight. "Good grief, I just did it again." The next step is likely to be middlesight. "There I was right in the middle of it and suddenly I knew what was going on!"

With persistence, the third step is foresight: "I really felt compelled to give her solutions and advice, but I managed not to." With enough foresight, games can be stopped before they start, hopefully in favor of a more authentic means of encounter.

Games can be broken up on either side. However, if we effectively thwart someone else's game, it is unrealistic to assume that the person is cured of game-playing.

That person is only cured of playing this game with us in the work situation. There is a high probability that the game will continue to be played elsewhere; a therapeutic change is often necessary for permanent change.

A knowledge of transactional analysis is a useful tool to give us more effective control over hurtful or wasteful interpersonal relationships on the job. In addition to helping us control what other people do to or with us, the application of TA helps us know ourselves. In fact, the most useful aspect of studying games in organizations is to give us more insight and control over our *own* games—those games we play in response to the people we work with and those encouraged by the organizational scripts. It isn't what we can do with or to the other person that always counts the most. It is what we learn about and are able to do about *ourselves.*

It is not uncommon for participants to discover that they themselves play some games. People who become aware of game-playing can either stop it, cut down the amount of time invested in it, or play at a less intense level.

Avoid the complementary hand. The classic way to thwart a game, of course, is not to play the expected complementary hand. Do something unexpected. Avoid giving or taking the negative payoff. For example, if a *Yes, But* player has you cornered, refuse to give advice or solutions to the stated problem. One method is to throw the problem back to the initiator of the game. Say perhaps, "It is a pretty rough problem, Harry. What are you going to do about it?"

It may be doubly hard to stop a *Yes, But* player if you play *I'm Only Trying to Help You.* These two games often fit, wasting considerable company time. In fact, anyone prone to collecting "kicks" may be easily suckered into *Yes, But.* Knowing the games we play helps us figure out what games of others' we fall into most easily.

For example, *I'm Only Trying to Help You* needs to be examined by anyone working for rescuing agencies or in the helping professions. If clients are not being cured, if illnesses are not being conquered, if social problems are not being alleviated, time is likely being invested in *I'm Only Trying to Help You* and/or *Ain't It Awful About Them* rather than solving problems.

Stop acting phony roles. One way to stop playing our own games is through an understanding of the roles we play. People may realize that they play a particular role more frequently than others. For example, some people gain insight into the fact that they often play-act at being a Victim. They use words, gestures, postures, and other behaviors to invite people to either persecute or rescue them. To stop games, stop play-acting at being a Victim. Stop play-acting at being a Persecutor. Stop play-acting at being a Rescuer.

Stop putting others down. Games always involve someone being put down—either one's self or someone else. One way to gain better control over one's own games is to become aware of, and refrain from, putting down or discounting others. Stop emphasizing other people's shortcomings. In a game of *Blemish*, for example, part of the ploy is to initiate feelings of guilt or inadequacy in the other person. Others are defined as not-OK, even though the game is usually a projection of the player's own sense of inadequacy.

The point of a put-down in a game may lie in different places within the game. For example, the game of *Uproar* starts with a put-down—usually a critical remark or gesture. Other games end with a put-down. Refraining from putting people down or defining them as insignificant helps to stop games.

As is suggested by McGregor's Theory X, some managers operate from a You're not-OK position. Consequently, they may tend to inhibit the growth of the people they manage. They are likely to play from the Persecutor role, act out games that put others down, and distribute negative stamps. TA can help to change that.

Stop putting yourself down. Negative feelings are either collected or distributed in all games. One way to help relieve the game-playing is to refrain from collecting negative feelings about yourself—feelings of inadequacy, fear, stupidity, anger, guilt, self-contempt, hurt and/or depression. Stop exaggerating personal shortcomings and practice accepting gold stamps.

D.S. discovered that every time someone tried to compliment her work, she warded off the compliment. Standard phrases she used were, "I would have been better if I'd had more time," "Gee, it wasn't anything," "Well, it could have been worse." Sometimes she would not only refuse to accept a gold stamp but would send back a gray stamp in return. For example, when she was complimented by her immediate supervisor for a report she had presented to management, she retorted, "You of all people ought to know that it could have been much better!"

In a TA training session she became very aware of her pattern and its effect on other people. Her parting shot in class was, "A simple 'thank you' is a lot easier than the antics I usually go through!"

Learn to accept positive strokes and give positive strokes. People who have learned to get most of their strokes by playing games will suffer feelings of stroke deprivation when they give them up. The task becomes one of getting positive strokes through alternative ways of structuring time. This often takes continuous practice, lengthening the time span between game encounters.

Some people will need to increase the number of

strokes they give and get through simple rituals. Even though rituals may be superficial ways of structuring time, nonetheless they supply people with maintenance strokes.

In addition, learning how to carry on a pastime with another person—simply talking about some innocuous subject—is an improvement over the hurtful interchange that a game involves. For any one person this means learning the facility of making small talk with other people. Such small talk might be centered around weather, travels, hobbies, schools once attended, favorite places to eat, etc. Too much time devoted to pastimes on the job can be inappropriate. However, a few pastimes are likely to be less destructive to the organization than games.

Rituals and pastimes provide low-intensity strokes which do not equal the intensity of game strokes. However, the quality of strokes through activities can be high if the job is enriched with intrinsic strokes. Therefore, more time needs to be invested in activities centered around getting the job done—productivity. Productivity feels good if it is tapping actual human potentials. People who learn to get and enjoy positive strokes by experiencing their unique potential through their work are winners.

People who learn to give more effective strokes to others are also winners. Negative patterns can be changed.

A not-OK position towards others can be modified at home as well as at work. The strokes we receive from intimacy are so intense that we "feel" them for a long time. You probably have experienced going back in your memories and reliving a special encounter with another person. If so, you may also have experienced the good feelings again.

Sometimes it's best to level. Risking authenticity is

sometimes difficult. However, leveling with another person about what you think is happening between you can sometimes clear the air. This is especially useful if you both know TA language. In any case, avoiding accusations raises the probability of being heard.

Management can help stop game-playing. There are many ways in which management can diminish the time invested in games. This can be encouraged by reducing boredom on the job; by enriching the work environment with positive strokes; and by allowing people to express and develop their own potentials (self-actualizing) so that they receive intrinsic strokes from their work by identifying personal goals and integrating them with organizational goals.

MARIA ARAPAKIS

Maria Arapakis is head of Arapakis Associates, a California-based consulting firm which designs and presents seminars internationally. As a psychologist, she has for the last twelve years applied her understanding of human behavior and attitudes to the world of business.

Maria has successfully worked with businesses ranging in size from Fortune 500 companies to small professional firms (and with levels of staff from Chief Executive Officer to secretary), to boost personal and corporate productivity. As a consultant, she helps clients with team-building, meeting management, role negotiations, partnership, and staff communications.

In addition to consulting work, Maria has designed and presented hundreds of professional seminars for managers, professionals, business owners, secretaries, and salespeople. Her seminar topics include "Speaking Your Mind: The Skills of Assertiveness," "Your Creative Mind: How to Tap into It," "What's on Your Mind?: The Inner Game of Success," and "Giving Work Away: The Art of Delegation."

Maria Arapakis was the youngest of three girls in her family and grew up on Long Island, New York. Valedictorian of her high-school class, Maria went on to graduate with high honors from the University of Rochester. During her undergraduate years she married, gave birth to her first son, David, and studied at the Sorbonne.

Following her graduation and the arrival of a second son, Mark, Maria and her family moved to California, where she now lives. Graduate and post-graduate work in Clinical and Educational Psychology at California State University, a year's internship at Letterman Army Hospital in San Francisco, and specialized training in family therapy, brain research, linguistics, and organization development make Maria well qualified to help those in business with the "people-side" of their work.

Maria believes strongly in positive thinking and an assertive approach to life. Best of all, she practices what she preaches with excellent results.

She is an active member of the American Business Association, the American Psychological Association, Organization Development Network, National Speakers Association, and the American Society of Training and Development. As a member of ASTD, she has been involved in the Community Training and Development Project, which brings consulting and seminars to nonprofit and community organizations at minimal expense.

You may contact Maria Arapakis at Arapakis Associates, 6121 Rock Ridge Boulevard So., Oakland, CA 94618. Telephone (415) 652-4452.

SETTING LIMITS:
THE ART OF SAYING NO
by MARIA ARAPAKIS

Dear Abby:
One of the women I work with is constantly talking about her sex life with her husband (she's not a young kid, either). Some of us are bored and others are embarrassed by her daily reports of what went on in her bedroom, but no one has the nerve to tell her. What should we do?

The Office Gang

Dear Gang:
If no one has the courage to speak up, you all deserve to be bored or embarrassed. You letter is a reminder that the meek are destined to put up with a lot.

Abby

Why is it so hard for people to set limits? In the communication seminars I've presented across the country, I invariably find participants—men and women alike—who lack the ability to say *no* comfortably and successfully. They have difficulty letting others know what they want and what they *don't* want, what they're willing to put up with and what they're *not* willing to put up with.

Setting limits is where you "draw the line," and, like it or not, we all must draw the line somewhere. We have, after all, only so much time and energy. How we use them determines both our success and our happiness. It's critical to make choices. Setting limits lets others know what our choices are so that they may respect them.

For some idea of the broad spectrum of situations in which limit-setting is an issue, consider this list.

- Someone asks you for a date and you're not interested.

- You're kept waiting for an engagement.

- You are dissatisfied with a meal or the table service.

- You think you're doing more than your share of the chores.

- You find out that someone has been gossiping about you.

- You're interrupted in the middle of important business.

- Someone shoves ahead of you in line.

- Someone belittles what you say at a meeting.

- You suspect a taxi driver of taking a roundabout route.

- Your doctor is not answering your questions satisfactorily.

- The bill at your repair shop is well over the estimate.

- Your child has been placed in the classroom of a seemingly incompetent teacher.

- Someone tells an offensive joke.

- Your host serves food you're allergic to.

- A friend overstays his welcome at your home.

- You're asked a personal question you don't want to answer.

- A friend wants to spend more time with you than you're willing to invest in the relationship.

And that's just the beginning! Setting limits is an issue we face dozens, maybe hundreds, of times each day.

WHY SET LIMITS, ANYWAY?

The need for setting limits may seem obvious to you. On the other hand, you may have never even given it a thought. Let's take a look at a few of the reasons why it makes sense to set limits.

Silence Implies Consent

If a friend consistently shows up a half-hour late and you say nothing, you communicate that it's OK with you to be kept waiting.

If someone persistently interrupts you midstream and you fail to say "I'd like to finish what I was saying," or "Please don't interrupt," the person may understandably assume that you don't mind being interrupted.

Whenever you don't speak up about behaviors that bother you, you send a silent message that implies consent. Other people cannot read your mind. You need to let them know *verbally* and *directly* when you're upset by their behavior.

Limits Are Individual

Our limits are as unique to each of us as our fingerprints. What bothers you doesn't necessarily bother someone else. Some people, for instance, enjoy having unexpected visitors drop by, while others find that upsetting. People are different.

I'm not comfortable lending my car to others. It makes no difference whether it's my teenage son or a close friend whom I trust to be a good driver—I'm willing to do it only in emergencies. But I know many people who lend their cars as easily as they lend a book. It doesn't bother them at all. Neither position is "right." They're merely different from each other.

Because limits vary so from individual to individual, never assume that others are aware of bothering you. They may see their behavior as totally acceptable and appropriate.

Limits Change Constantly

Our limits are in a constant state of flux, depending on how we feel at a given moment, with whom we're interacting, what time of day it is, and where we are. And furthermore, what you're willing to accept today isn't necessarily what you're willing to accept tomorrow or three months from now. You might be busier then. Or ill. Or traveling. Your limits will change accordingly.

I may be willing to accept certain behavior under one set of circumstances but not under another. A casual phone call at 3 a.m. is not OK with me. But in the case of an emergency it would be quite acceptable.

Similarly, informal table manners may be appropriate in your family breakfast room, but unacceptable at a fine restaurant.

These are excellent reasons why we must let other people know where our limits are and not expect them to guess. Because limits depend on circumstances, setting them is an on-going process, not a one-time event.

Not Setting Limits Doesn't Work

This may be the most compelling reason to make limit-setting a daily part of your life. When you fail to set limits, instead of solving problems you invite new ones. You experience one or more of these results:

- You're likely to go about trying to get what you want *indirectly.*

- You end up doing a lot of things you don't want to do.

- You end up *not* doing a lot of things you *do* want to do.

- Problems repeat themselves.

- Relationships suffer.

Indirect communication is inefficient at its best, ineffective and self-defeating at its worst. There are many subtle ways of being indirect about what you want. Perhaps you criticize ("You talk too much") instead of asking for what you want directly ("I'd like you to listen to me. I want my time to talk, too").

Or maybe you manipulate ("You deserve a nice night out") rather than communicating in a straightforward way ("I'd like to go out to eat tonight").

Know that being direct about what you want can be uncomfortable and risky at first, but pays enormous dividends. When you do not establish what your limits are, you may spend most of your time and energy responding to what others want for you and from you rather than on what you want for yourself. If you don't decide what you want and assert yourself, *someone else will decide for you!*

It's plain common sense that if others are not told when they've bothered you, they're likely to bother you again and again in the same way. If you don't tell drop-in visitors, "Next time, I'd appreciate a phone call before you stop by," you can bet they'll come by unexpectedly again, and perhaps they'll leave wondering why you seemed so cool and aloof.

Relationships suffer when you don't set limits. Resentments build: You feel taken advantage of. You judge others to be inconsiderate and rude, and you feel like a victim. Failure to set limits is unhealthy for individuals and relationships alike.

THE OBSTACLES

Given all these good reasons, how is it that setting limits is so hard for so many to do so much of the time? What typically prevents people from setting limits?

Lack of Awareness

One large factor inhibiting limit-setting is lack of awareness. In order to set limits, you obviously need to know what your limits are and when they've been crossed. Problems with awareness show themselves in a variety of ways.

Total oblivion. If you are completely unaware of what you want and don't want, it's obvious that you will fail to set limits. If this is a lifelong pattern, you eventually get a bleeding ulcer, high blood pressure, or cancer. Cancer research has demonstrated the existence of a cancer-prone personality, someone described by family and friends as a "saint," always doing for others rather than for self. This person sacrifices his or her own needs, and often feels like a victim in the process.

While this represents the extreme, there is always a high price to pay for a life-style of self-sacrifice. At best, you are perpetually overextended, worn to a frazzle.

Delayed awareness. In this case you do notice that your limit has been crossed, but you do so after the fact and, most importantly, you fail to do anything about it (except perhaps gripe and complain to a third party). You automatically say *yes* to requests and invitations, only to regret it a few minutes later. You allow yourself to be mistreated, only to feel enraged after it's over. If this sort of thing occurs with you, take heart, for it's only when you're aware of a problem that you can do anything about it.

Confused awareness. At times you may have problems setting limits because you get confused by mixed feelings. Problems with limits are primarily signaled by *feelings.* Yet feelings are complex and can be hard to understand. You can experience a multitude of emotions simultaneously and have difficulty sorting them out. For instance, you might feel flattered, curious, annoyed, pleased, pressured, overextended, and anxious at being asked to chair an important committee, and be unable to decide which feeling to follow.

To make matters even more challenging, you can also experience complex and conflicting *intentions.* You may want incompatible things. At the same time, you may want and *not* want to chair the committee. Unless you are clear about which intention takes priority (that is, which you want the most), you're likely to do what's lower on your list without even realizing it.

While awareness is necessary for successful limit-setting, it is not in itself *sufficient.* As you well know, you may be all too aware of a violated limit yet do nothing about it.

Fear

Often it is fear that prevents you from enforcing your limits. Fear is a major obstacle. Sometimes it's fear of hurting someone's feelings. Or of creating a scene. Fear of rejection, fear of disapproval, fear of loss of friendship, fear of an angry reaction, fear of being called "selfish" or "difficult" are items on a seemingly endless list.

Fortunately, many of these fears are set in motion by non-assertive beliefs which you have the ability to change. You may fear disapproval because you believe you must have the approval of everyone at all times. You may fear an angry reaction because you don't believe you can deal with it effectively.

Overcoming these fears is a two-step process. First, you need to identify the beliefs that are fueling the feelings. Second, you need to *change the beliefs*. Reading positive thinking books can help in turning self-defeating beliefs into self-fulfilling ones.

Forgetting Basic Rights

A third obstacle to limit-setting is the failure to accept for yourself certain basic, inalienable human rights. If you don't believe you have the right to decide how to spend your time, you'll have a hard time turning down invitations you don't want to accept.

Other basic rights to keep in mind when setting limits are:

- The right to choose your own lifestyle.
- The right to ask for what you want.
- The right to make an honest mistake.

- The right to set the priorities in your life.
- The right to have time alone when you need it.
- The right to take time to think.
- The right to change your mind.
- The right to ask questions.

Needless to say, there are many other rights. They constitute a set of attitudes reflecting responsibility as well as freedom in determining your behaviors with others. For each right, there is a matching responsibility. For example, while I may have the right to an honest mistake, I don't have the right to make a reckless one. For each right I automatically incur responsibility for the consequences of my behavior.

No Skills

Lack of skills is the fourth obstacle to limit-setting. You can be keenly aware of your need to set limits and fully accepting of your right to do so, yet have no idea how to go about doing it. Let's face it, most of us grew up around people with limit-setting problems worse than our own. We had no one to learn from.

Many of our mothers were caretakers who thought of everyone but themselves. Many of our fathers set limits arbitrarily, without considering others' viewpoints and feelings. It's not surprising that many of us grew up believing we had one of two choices: to allow others to step all over us or to step all over them first.

Let's look now at what it takes to set limits skillfully, without resorting to either of these extremes.

GUIDELINES

Limit-setting often has to be accomplished at a time when emotions are running high. Because we often temporarily lose our ability to think clearly and rationally at such times, it's important to have a clear mental picture of how to set limits effectively. To give you a mental model, let's explore some guidelines for limit-setting.

1. Let Your Feelings Help You

Feelings are often the first indication that you need to set limits. Welcome your upset feelings as a valuable reminder that there's a problem that needs your attention.

If I answer the phone during dinner and then feel restless and irritated by the interruption, I can use those feelings to remind myself of my primary intentions to eat a hot meal and to have a relaxed visit with my sons. Once reminded, I can say pleasantly, "I'd like to visit, but right now I'm in the middle of dinner. When can I call you back?"

Using your feelings in this way, as limit-indicators, involves asking yourself some questions:

- What are my feelings?
- What are my feelings a response to?
- How is this situation a problem for me?
- What do I really want in this situation? (And what do I *not* want?)
- Is there some basic right I need to remind myself of?

2. Learn to Be Specific

The more specific you can be in describing your limits to others, the more they'll be able to respect them. Determine *exactly* what's bothering you and why. Is it your friend's lateness, or the fact he didn't call ahead of time to tell you he'd be late?

Determine *exactly* what you're willing to do. Are you willing to drive your son to his party only if he has no other way to get there? Put out exactly what you want and don't want. It makes it easier for others to cooperate.

I am a punctual person who expects others to respect time agreements. I have a friend who used to call me at 9:10 to tell me she was just leaving for our 9:00 appointment and would be a half-hour late. She thought she was being considerate in calling, but by the time she called I'd already put out extra effort to be ready on time. I felt resentful that I hadn't known earlier.

I finally told my friend that I'd like her to anticipate her lateness and call me ahead of time, so I could use my time to best advantage. Being specific helped her to understand what I wanted from her and why.

3. Remember to Use Partial Limits

Using partial limits is tied to being specific. The point to keep in mind is that setting limits does not have to be an all-or-nothing proposition: "Yes, I'll do it" or "No, I won't."

There are many situations in which you may be willing to do a part of what's requested or expected but not all of it. Here are some examples of partial limits:

- "I'd love to go out for dinner, but I really don't want to go anyplace where I need to dress up."

- "I'm willing to accept this dress with the spot on it, but I'd want some reduction in the price."

- "I don't mind staying another 15 or 20 minutes, but then I'd like to go home. I feel really tired."

- "Yes, I'd like to chair the committee, but only if I have access to a support staff to take care of the paperwork."

- "Mom, I'd love to come by for dinner later but I'll have to leave by 9:30."

4. Take Time to Think

A friend of mine has an especially tough time setting limits. He suffers from delayed awareness and has learned the hard way not to trust his first response to requests and invitations. Whenever possible, he'll take at least a few minutes before responding to reflect on what he really wants and what his priorities are.

People often respond impulsively (and frequently in ways counter to what they really want), out of some sense of pressure. They feel obligated to answer immediately. Later, they either try to get out of the commitment they've made with an excuse or, perhaps worse, they follow through with a half-hearted, resentful effort.

When you begin making more considered responses, friends will find that they can count on you for whole-hearted follow-through.

5. Act Rather Than React

It's often easier to be effective in setting limits when you don't do it at the scene of the problem. Rather than wait for the friend who has been calling you too early in the morning to strike again, bring the subject up during a friendly lunch. Or mention it casually the next time you see the person.

There are several reasons why this makes sense, but the main one is that you will not be reacting emotionally to the problem behavior while you are trying to communicate your limits.

Anticipatory limit-setting also works well in situations in which you foresee the need to set a limit in the near future. Setting it ahead of time is often easier and more effective than waiting till the problem arises. Here are some examples:

- "I have about five more minutes to talk. Then I'll have to get back to work."

- "I want to hear what I've done that's made you angry, but I don't want you yelling at me."

- "I'd love to go to the movies, but I won't be able to go out afterwards. I want to be home by 11:30."

Anticipatory limit-setting is considerate of others, as it gives them a chance to react to your limit *before the fact*. In the last example, your friend might suggest you meet at the movies, so you can go your separate ways afterward.

6. Use Appropriate Muscle Levels

Some people consistently fail to set limits, only to blow up in anger after their "patience" runs out. Part of their problem, of course, comes from keeping their limits a secret, all the while hoping others will read the nonverbal, indirect messages they are sending out. The eventual angry outburst is an example of inappropriate "muscle level."

A secretary once complained to me that no one in her office took her seriously. She had announced at a staff meeting, for example, that she was no longer available for filling out routine medical forms. Yet, day after day she continued to be approached with requests and pleas for help from those she knew could help themselves. I pointed out to her that the only person needing to take her limits seriously was herself. To show others that she meant what she said, she would have to increase her muscle level.

She needed to follow-up her initial announcement with firm yet pleasant refusals to fill out forms. If the requests continued, she might have resorted to a yet stronger message. Only by taking herself seriously would she teach others to take her seriously.

Muscle level one. Muscle level one assumes that others are not intentionally trying to upset you. It gives others the benefit of the doubt and assumes that once aware of the problem, they'll respond in a considerate, cooperative way.

Muscle level one is simply a low-level statement of what you want or don't want. In a situation where you find yourself being interrupted, you might say "Excuse me, but I'd like to finish what I was saying."

Unfortunately, others don't always respond to such low-level assertions the way you'd like them to. This can be most disheartening and is the point at which many who are new at limit-setting get discouraged. You had the courage to speak up, but it didn't seem to make any difference.

Muscle level two. When you face such a situation, you need to "up" your muscle level. Muscle level two involves increasing the intensity of your message. You repeat your limit with voice tone and volume, body language, and eye-contact all saying "I'm serious about this message." At this level you might say "I do *not* want to be interrupted!"

Muscle level three. On the rare occasions when others continue to violate your limit, you need to use level three. Muscle level three lets other people know what action you will take and what consequences there will be if they fail to respect your limit. You're going to give them one last chance to change their behavior.

At this level you might say, "The next time you interrupt me, I'll consider this discussion finished."

Muscle level four. On the few occasions when a higher level of muscle is called for, it's extremely important to follow through with action. Level four involves doing what you said you'd do. If you fail to follow through, you teach people that you don't mean what you say.

You might be tempted to tell the kids fighting in the back seat at the start of a two-week camping trip, "If you don't cut it out, we're not going to go camping!" That would sound good but be hard to act on. A more reasonable consequence would be that of pulling over to the curb till the fighting stops.

It's sometimes hard to know what you'll do as a level-four consequence. The consequence must be both suitable to the situation and realistic.

7. Set "Meta-level" Limits

Once in a while you must set limits *as you are setting limits.* This occurs when others respond to your limit-setting in an unacceptable way. A friend recently told me of a dismaying experience she had at work. A co-worker spoke to her in an offensive manner during a staff meeting, and while she was trying to tell him how she felt about it, he gave every appearance of not listening. She found it increasingly difficult to continue talking about his behavior during the meeting when his behavior *right then* was a problem for her.

She needed to set "meta-level" limits (limits regarding the here-and-now problem she was experiencing). It might have gone something like this: "I can't tell if you're listening to me. You seem very distracted. It's important to me that you hear and understand what I'm saying. Can I have your full attention?"

8. Separate Intent From Results

The best intentions can result in negative outcomes. Sometimes you're reluctant to set limits with others because you believe their intentions are good ones and you don't want to offend them or hurt their feelings. When this occurs, say that directly. Tell them that while you assume they mean well, you're still having trouble with their behavior, and you want something different from them:

- "I assume you just want to be helpful, but I really do want to finish this job on my own."

- "You probably haven't been aware that this was bothering me, but I'd prefer a phone call before you drop by."

- "I know your intentions are good, but I'm not ready to hear what you're telling me. I'd like to hear this later."

On the other hand, *your* good intentions may be occasionally misinterpreted. For this reason it sometimes helps to state what your intentions are *not*, as well as what they are:

- "I don't mean to be rude—I just don't feel like talking right now."

- "I'm not trying to criticize you or tell you how to live your life. I do need to tell you, however, that I'm not willing to cover for you when you come to work late."

- "I don't mean to rush you, but I feel ill and would like to leave as soon as we can."

- "I want to prevent hard feelings from building. That's why I'm bringing this up."

9. Don't Try to Justify Your Limits

Although you may need to share the reasoning behind your limits, beware of engaging in point-counter-point arguments on limits that are not open for negotiation.

When you present your reasons for setting a limit, the other person involved will sometimes infer from continuing discussion that the issue is still open to argument. If, in fact, your limit *is* negotiable, this is fine. But, when it's not, you may find yourself getting caught up in something like this:

"Mommy, why can't we buy this cereal?"

"Because it's too expensive."

"It's not that expensive. It's not any more money than this kind you said we could get."

"It is *so* expensive! The box is much smaller! Besides, it's junk food—all sugar. Put it back!"

"It's not junk, Mom. It's got vitamins and minerals. Look—it says so here on the box!"

"You can't believe everything you read on boxes. It's *junk!* We're not buying it."

"Judy buys it, and she wouldn't buy junk, would she?"

"Just put it back!"

You get the picture. It's not necessary to justify every decision you make with indisputable reasons.

10. Don't Encourage Behavior You Dislike

A friend who happens to be a terrific listener complains that some of her friends talk too much, never giving her a chance to tell *her* stories. I had the chance to see her in action at a dinner party. She gave her companion total, undivided attention, alternating between avid listening and enthusiastic questions. She made Barbara Walters look like a light-weight. Small wonder the guy never stopped talking! How could he have known my friend was feeling frustrated and resentful that she didn't get a turn to talk? Through her behavior she was unknowingly reinforcing and encouraging the very behavior that was bothering her.

11. Beware of Using Excuses

Excuses, like reasons, can work against you. If the excuse is not legitimate, you may find that you've painted yourself into a corner you can't get out of. (What if your friend says, "Oh, don't worry about getting a sitter! There's babysitting available at the center"?)

This young mother's story tells more about how excuses create problems. "If I find myself in a situation that I can't handle honestly, for fear of hurting someone's feelings, I always use my children as a way out. For instance, I've often turned down invitations by saying, 'Gee, something's come up with one of my children and I won't be able to go with you.'

"I don't know how long I'll be able to do that, because the more independent my children become, the less they're going to be around for me to use that way. I'm worried that I'll never be an honest, forthright person— for my entire adult life I've formulated excuses to avoid situations.

"My mother never spoke ill of anybody in her whole life. Yet that sort of person loses credibility. *I don't want to be that kind of person,* but I'm aware that I'm critical about people only behind their backs. I can never come out and tell somebody how I really feel!"

Excuses, of course, are also the age-old way women have turned down unwelcome dates. Women who do this know all too well how excuses tend to catch up with them. There comes the time when he says, "Well, when *are* you free?" and you're left having to admit your bluff or give in.

•

Hopefully, these guidelines will enable you to set limits more effectively. Begin by applying them to situations of the least emotional impact and consequence. As you gain confidence in your ability to define your limits effectively, practice applying them in more critical situations.

While these guidelines will help you be a better limit-setter in many situations, they won't prevent all problems from arising. Learning to be direct and honest about your limits is a road filled with never-ending challenges. The best way to keep yourself on the path is to remind yourself of the enormous price you pay when you fail to set limits for yourself and of the equally great benefits you gain when you do set them!

Each day is yours, to do with as you will. This is both your *right* and your *responsibility*.

MARILYNN NIXON

Marilynn Nixon is a woman of warmth, openness, and courage. Her contagious enthusiasm and optimistic approach to life's challenges draw people to her programs. Participants leave her workshops, seminars, and speeches with renewed spirit.

Marilynn draws on the richness of life experiences—from small-town girl to city woman, from wife and mother to career woman. She has been in front of crowds ever since she sang "Away in a Manger" to a church congregation at the age of five. The soloist in that small church in Illinois is today a convention speaker and seminar leader who has spoken to groups as large as 700.

Among the topics Marilynn enjoys presenting are "Change, Loss, Joy," "Women's Hats," and "Goal-

Setting." She understands change, joy, and loss and sees them all as a natural part of life. She sees coping with change and finding joy as a major challenge of our time.

"Women's Hats" has to do with women's roles. The ability to help others understand the balancing act and pressures on women today is one of Marilynn's special gifts.

Goal-setting has worked in Marilynn's career and brought her where she is today. When she talks about goals and time-management, she speaks from experience. Her career has spanned a number of fields, from retail and education to medical. She is genuinely interested in people, and this is reflected in everything she does. A frequent television and radio talk-show guest, Marilynn is comfortable in every setting.

Marilynn Nixon can be contacted by writing to her at 6705 Cheltenham, Houston, TX 77096; or telephone (713) 771-2065.

MAKE ROOM FOR JOY

SOMETIMES IT COMES FROM SORROW

by MARILYNN NIXON

We live in a time of extremely rapid change, and it often leaves our minds reeling, our emotions on edge, our bodies exhausted, our spirits depleted. There is another result of this ever-increasingly accelerating change. It forces us to face grief daily.

Actually, the whole change process is analogous to death in some ways, and brings sorrow along with its advantages. With each new aspect of life, each innovation, each improvement, something old and familiar passes away. The Watergate issue, for example, sent our whole society into grief over the passing of the country we had known and loved. We recognized that our national image had changed and things would never be the same again.

Routine grief can assume such a major part in our

lives that we see only the dark side of life. What I am inviting you to do is recognize that we all need to deal with our grief so that we can make room for joy. I believe that this is one of the greatest needs in today's world.

Alvin Toffler coined another term for this grief I am talking about. He called it "future shock." We have experienced more change and growth in this century than at any other time in the world's history. There is change on every hand. My grandfather, who was born in the late 1800s, came all the way from the covered wagon days to seeing man walk on the moon. Yet the change of perhaps the greatest emotional impact came with the Vietnam War when, for the first time, we saw real people dying on television. We saw our own people dying as well as the enemy. It was difficult then to ignore the fact that people do die, that death has a part in day-to-day life.

Our society has not wanted to deal with issues of grief, death, and dying, and yet in the last 20 years it's been almost impossible for us to ignore those realities. With the assassinations of the Kennedys, Martin Luther King, Jr., Mayor Moscone of San Francisco, and the mass murders in California, Illinois, and Texas, the American people have had to face up to the fact of death.

I have been studying and working with death and dying and the grief process. The process of dealing with the loss of a loved one is equally applicable to the other kinds of losses that accompany change. The foremost research in this field has been done by Elisabeth Kubler-Ross, M.D. In her books on death and dying, she talks about the necessity of taking care of unfinished business. By this she means maintaining relationships with others at a high level and keeping them current. This includes mending broken relationships, telling people you love them, and bringing appropriate closure. Living in close proximity to death certainly increases our ability to deal with the here-and-now and not put things off.

Once you have accepted the finiteness of man and realize that you are not going to live forever on this earth, you move into a different plane. I have experienced that for myself. We can have closer, more human relationships. There is increased sharing, and it includes both griefs and joys. Sharing both ends of the spectrum helps build rainbow bridges between us and others along life's way.

Let's examine the grief process. The difference between the person diagnosed as terminally ill and the rest of us is that he or she has been given a deadline—only six months to live, only three years to live. That person may die much sooner than that. So may you or I, although we have been given no such warning—it's always possible to be suddenly struck down by an accident, a tornado, or a fatal heart attack. But we seldom plan on it.

There are a lot of advantages to having a deadline. I have known several people who lived their last days more fully than I ever dreamed possible. They determined what was important for them and they spent the time and energy they had left on those most important things.

When my mother-in-law, Fay, was diagnosed as being terminally ill with leukemia, she chose not to undergo chemotherapy or any other life-prolonging attempts. Fay was 73 at the time, had lived a long life, and had been alone as a widow for the last 20 years. She had emphysema, and various other old-age diseases as well, and felt that she was certain to die of one of them in a short while. We discussed her illness openly as a family and all agreed that in her case treatment for the cancer would simply postpone the inevitable.

On one of Fay's better days, my sister-in-law and I had taken her by wheelchair to the hospital cafeteria. We sat at a table near a window, where she could look out at the rose garden in the park across the street.

As we chatted and watched people come and go, Fay brought up the subject of her funeral. She started naming the people she wanted to serve as pallbearers. Since several of the people she named were not familiar to me, I got out a note pad and wrote them down. Then she said to me, "What about your children? Would the two boys be willing to serve as pallbearers?"

I said, "My goodness, I don't know. I'll certainly ask them."

And she said, "What about your Dad? Would he be willing to be a pallbearer?"

I said, "I don't know. He isn't in very good health, but it's certainly worth asking him. I'll check it out."

I had no idea that she would have chosen the three of them. I was so glad we had been given the incentive to work out the arrangements and find out her exact wishes.

The family also has the advantage of spending more time with the dying person, and they can say goodbye in their own way. It's important to say goodbye to someone you've loved and cared about. It's important to both of you to say all the things you would like for them to hear. And this all serves as your first step in adjusting to the idea of life without this very special person.

My grandfather was a remarkable man. He worked until he was 65, like most men of that day, and then decided to retire. He stayed home only about six months before deciding that retirement was not for him. Then he went back to work, and he worked until he was 85.

When my grandfather was about 92, my father and I were discussing the fact that he had worked right through what most people would consider their retirement. My dad said to him, "Pop, what do you call this part of your life?"

My grandfather kind of grinned and looked out the

window and said, "Well, I call this 'waiting for the chariot to pull up out front.'" Even this was a special time of life for Pop and those who loved him.

In those last few years my grandfather and I had several chances to chat about what we meant to each other and how much of an inspiration he had been to me. When he told me how wonderful I was, I loved to tell him that I came from good stock.

Since I have been involved with death and dying and grief issues, I try to sustain the awareness that each day may be my last day. I now try to live each day as I would want to live it if I had only six months to live. And living this way has brought a lot of joy into my life.

Steps to Acceptance

It is helpful to know the stages that a terminally ill person goes through in moving toward acceptance of death. These stages have been noted and discussed by Dr. Elisabeth Kubler-Ross.

Denial. After the initial shock wears off, the patient experiences a condition of isolation and denial—denial of being terminally ill, denial that the diagnosis is correct. He may consult doctor after doctor in search of one who will say, "The diagnosis was wrong. You're going to be okay." The patient chooses to spend most of his time by himself during this stage, and may do a lot of head-shaking. One young woman I know who was diagnosed as having cancer refused to say the word. It was as if she believed she could invalidate the diagnosis by rejecting the word.

Another dear friend admitted to being terminal and yet denied the seriousness and extent of her illness. In her case, that partial denial kept her extremely productive until the week before her death.

Anger. The second phase, says Kubler-Ross, is anger—anger at family, friends, God, and anyone close at hand. The dying person may be very difficult to get along with at this time.

One man became very sarcastic and hostile with his anger. He made cutting remarks toward anyone within hearing. Some days at work he slammed doors, threw books and papers, and then drove home recklessly. These actions were all manifestations of the anger he felt at moving toward death.

Bargaining. The third stage is wanting to bargain. The bargaining is usually with God. It may take the form of "If you'll just give me six more months, I'll be nice to Richard," or "Whatever you want me to do, God, I'll do it—if you just let me live a little while longer." The person who is bargaining may spend a good deal of time alone in quiet meditation.

Depression. As the person realizes that the bargaining did not work, he turns his anger and frustration inward, becoming depressed. "There's no way out," he might say. Or with fading hope, he may withdraw. The depressed person sleeps an excessive amount and discontinues his daily routines. His thoughts and conversations might express "getting it over with." Spells of crying generally accompany depression along with little care for personal grooming.

Acceptance. Finally, the patient moves into the stages of acceptance. Though the person may still want very much to be well and to live, he fully accepts the fact of his impending death. A sense of peace becomes apparent at this point, and the patient is released to begin taking care of unfinished business.

It is during this stage that a person, like my mother-in-law, Fay, will plan his funeral. He will be likely to want to spend time with loved ones and dear friends, and he will grow increasingly reflective about the meaning of life and his existence as a part of life.

Peace comes with acceptance and a person in acceptance will do more "caretaking" than the people around him.

Although these are described as five separate steps, a patient may move back and forth through them intermittently, from denial to acceptance to bargaining and back to acceptance. Sometimes it may seem to onlookers that one stage has been by-passed entirely.

Kubler-Ross says that these steps to acceptance are universally experienced by the terminally ill. They somewhat resemble the process experienced by the family after the person dies. I believe that we go through this grief process anytime we lose something or someone we love and even when there are other major positive changes in our lives.

It is also my experience that anyone who starts looking at the meaning of life and death goes through these stages. Like most of us, I spent my days in denial—until I developed a friendship with Beth. Beth had cancer when I met her. During the years she battled cancer we moved from acquaintanceship to being good friends.

As our friendship deepened, I became angry. I asked why she should have to suffer and struggle so? Why should I have to lose a good friend—such a talented woman and one who taught me a lot about my life and work? I was really angry!

At one point, I couldn't stand the thought of losing her. I had to come to an understanding of the meaning of her life and my life. I withdrew. I could not stand my emotional pain when I was with her and saw her struggling with emotional and physical pain.

During my withdrawal, I spent many lonely hours

reading and thinking. Finally I came to grips with my feelings of life and death.

I still very much wanted Beth to live. She had so much knowledge and I still wanted to learn more from her. One day at lunch, with tears in my eyes, I said, "Beth, it's okay with me for you to die. I'd very much like for you to live to be a very old lady, but I'll be okay if that doesn't happen." She smiled at me with tears in her eyes.

Both of us knew that what I had said to her revealed a great deal about myself. I had reached an understanding of life and felt acceptance—*truly* felt it—for the very first time.

I think that since then I have been a more effective, loving, and sharing person. Learning acceptance has made it possible for me to deal with what I call "dumb and ugly" days, those days when my whole world seems to go wrong.

The Grief Process

I find it useful to view the grief process as having three major aspects: shock and emotional release, acute grief, and renewal.

Release. First, let's take a look at shock and emotional release. Shock is like a cocoon that surrounds the person who has been exposed to something too painful to bear. Walled off as in an isolation chamber, the person does not experience the emotions of the trauma at this stage. The emotional release, such as tears, comes later. People often need to be told that it's really okay to express their emotions. The person who does not cry at the funeral will eventually have a more difficult time coming to terms with the loss.

Recently a woman who heard of my "Living with Dying" seminar called to talk about her grief. She and her two-year-old son had been in a fire a year ago. The child had mercifully died. She was hospitalized at the time of his funeral and had not expressed her sorrow. Now, slightly over a year since the child's death, she still had not cried. She knew that she was keeping her emotions bottled up and that deep inside she had a volcano of grief.

Grief. Acute grief, when it surfaces, is made up of many emotions. It starts with depression and loneliness, and it sometimes includes physical symptoms. It is when a person has not expressed his emotions and moved through the grief process that psychosomatic illnesses such as headaches, backaches, and ulcers become a problem.

Sometimes a grieving person may actually feel as if he is shaking both on the inside and the outside. This feeling may be accompanied by resentment and hostility. At that stage the person will lash out at others and may begin to feel as if he will never again live a normal life. He may think, "I can't go back to work. I can't even go to the grocery store. I'm unable to do anything."

One day while I was walking through the halls of Hermann Hospital in Houston, an elderly woman stopped me to ask directions. She had come to have tests done. Her husband had died of heart disease three weeks before and now she believed she had the same thing. Later I reflected on how the onset of her illness was close-ly tied to his death.

Renewal. Then slowly, gradually, renewal of spirit begins. Joy reappears. It's like finding a small dim light at the end of a tunnel, and watching it grow brighter. The person begins to adjust to the loss, and gain confidence in new ways of functioning. The trauma is over.

In the case of the death of a loved one, it sometimes takes as much as a year to get through the first cycle of grief. Every holiday or special occasion becomes a reminder of the absent loved one. From what I've heard, loss of a close relationship through divorce is probably more difficult than through death—the ever-present glimmer of hope for reconciliation serves as an obstacle to acceptance.

Room for Joy

Now that we have considered the sources of grief in our lives and processes for moving through it, what about joy? I believe that after you make room for joy by acknowledging and moving through your grief, there are steps you can take to bring more joy into your life.

Many people seem to think that joy consists of a hyped-up kind of rah-rah energy. I see that as a denial of reality. My experience of joy is a *solid* feeling, a kind of affirmation of life that holds me up even in times of grief or despair. It is peace.

Joy is an integral part of my life, which increases and decreases, which rides the ups and downs, but which is sustaining. I believe that the key to experiencing joy lies in caring for the *whole* of our beings—body, mind, spirit, and emotions.

First, get in touch with your body. If you're feeling bad emotionally, if you don't get proper food and rest and exercise, then your body feels bad. When your body feels bad, then the rest of you is apt to feel bad. One of the essentials in moving on to joy in your life is to take good care of your body. Get proper nourishment, rest, and exercise. This is important to feeling good about yourself.

Second, be aware of the needs of your mind. You must have meaning in your daily life; you must do something bigger than yourself, be committed to something.

Sigmund Freud, when asked what life was all about, said, "We're to love and work."

Meaningful work and loving other people are important to being a joyful human being. Do something to stretch and challenge your mind. I have found it helpful to be with people who are intellectually stimulating. Some of my best creative thinking happens when I am talking or working with a friend who is in touch with her own creativity.

Third, strengthen the emotional part of your life. Develop a good network of friends. It has been said that more good therapy is accomplished over a cup of coffee in someone's kitchen than on all of the psychiatrist's couches in the world. Having had friends who helped me through some of my emotional trauma, I can certainly agree with that.

A recent report confirms that one of the best methods of alleviating stress is to pick up the phone and call a friend.

Finally, pay attention to your spiritual life. Incorporate some form of daily meditation into your daily routine. Whether you read some kind of timeless material—such as Shakespeare, Plato, Aristotle, the Bible, the Koran—or whether you practice transcendental meditation or whether you look at a fiery sunset is unimportant. But do something for your spirit every day.

You are the caretaker of your whole self. Strive to maintain a balance between your body, mind, emotions, and spirit. Take care of these four areas as if you were a gardener tending a plot of rare and valuable specimens. Because you are unique and your life is unique, only you can make room for more joy in your life.

Some of the ways I sow joy in my life include reading, observing sunsets, visiting with friends, exercising, eating good food, and creating things with my hands. I give myself an abundance of quiet time. I take care of me. I know that if I do not take care of myself, I will not have anything to give to anyone else.

Learn to savor the meaning of the moment. Be aware of daily joys. Get in the habit of *looking* for joy in both the little things of life and the overall fabric of life. When you search for joy, you may find it in unexpected places:

Lord, make me an instrument of Thy peace . . .
where there is hatred, let me sow love,
where there is injury, pardon;
where there is doubt, faith;
where there is despair, hope;
where there is darkness, light;
and where there is sadness, joy.
O Divine Master,
grant that I may not so much
seek to be consoled as to console;
to be understood as to understand;
to be loved as to love;
for it is in giving that we receive;
it is in pardoning that we are pardoned;
and it is in dying that we
are born to eternal life.

—St. Francis of Assisi

DICK and GLORIA COBB

Dick and Gloria Cobb offer a unique program as a husband-and-wife speaking team. They share a fascinating, humorous/serious look at their marriage and why it works so well. Their presentation, "Cobb and Company" has been acclaimed by audiences throughout the country.

Business, education, and religious groups have heard their discussion of the three key factors for a successful marriage. Their talk is loaded with practical examples and delivered in an entertaining style.

Gloria Cobb is recognized as one of the most dynamic women on the platform today. Her unique presentation, "Wrap Your Own Package," helps people look better as well as feel better. She appears regularly on the NBC affiliate program *A New Day,* which is telecast from Milwaukee. She was recently featured in the *Milwaukee Journal* as one of the "ten top talkers" in Wisconsin.

Dick Cobb has worked in education at all levels, elementary grades through college. A recipient of a National Defense Act grant to do graduate work at the University of Wisconsin, he is now an administrator in a suburban Milwaukee school system.

In addition to managing Gloria's speaking career, Dick is an active lay leader in the Elmbrook Church. He and Gloria travel on weekends and throughout the summer months to present "Cobb and Company." They are the parents of two teenage children.

You can contact Dick and Gloria Cobb by writing to 3318 N. Knoll Boulevard, Milwaukee, WI 53222; or telephone (414) 259-0959.

HOW TO LOVE
BEING MARRIED

---

by DICK and GLORIA
COBB

We were sitting in the famous Sardi's Restaurant in New York City, guests of *Woman's Day* magazine in which Gloria was being featured in a series of articles. During the luncheon conversation one of the editors asked "To what do you attribute your happy marriage?" Her question surprised us, and my answer probably seemed unimpressive.

Since that time we've had a lot of time to think about that question: What does make a happy marriage? A lot of people are asking that question today.

It is interesting to note that more than 50,000 people responded to a national survey conducted by a popular magazine. The questionnaire asked: "If you had it to do all over again, would you marry the same person?" The respondents answered 48 percent *yes* and 52 percent *no*. More than half were not happy with their mates. What devastating commentary on marriage American-style!

A newspaper reporter recently interviewed a famous couple about their impending marital breakup. Theirs had been a "model" marriage. When the reporter asked why they were separating, the couple replied, "We're simply bored to death with one another. We have everything we want and we don't want anything we have."

It's so true. If you have a dream, you have everything. If you have everything and no dream then everything means nothing.

Dick: One of the fall-out effects of modern living is the high divorce rate. It strikes good friends and members of our own families. Happily married couples who Gloria and I thought were perfectly matched have suddenly announced to us that they were splitting. In my job as an elementary school principal I'm often visited by parents who say, "Please be patient with my children. We're getting a divorce and it's pretty upsetting to them. As a matter of fact, it's a shock to me, too."

I wondered about the causes of such widespread failing relationships. It occurred to me that if it happens to others, couldn't it happen to Gloria and me? What can a couple do to protect their marriage? What red flags should one be aware of?

We took a look at our marriage. We examined our relationship: What is the glue that holds us together? What makes our marriage vital, exciting, and rich? What causes a marriage to flourish and keeps it growing? We tried to identify those influences that make a relationship prosperous and secure.

We came up with three basic principles and three simple key words to exemplify them. First, we found it's important for a marriage to have GOALS. A couple needs shared goals. And individuals within the relationship need personal goals.

Second, you need to identify and clarify your respective ROLES. What is each member expected to do?

Third, nurture your SOUL. This is the part that ties it all together.

We never determined at the beginning of our marriage, 25 years ago, that it would be built on these three elements. In retrospect it appears that these ideas and values became evident only as we dealt with issues and problems and questions that came up in the course of our relationship. We became consciously aware of them then, and subsequently they became part of our subconscious behavior.

Yes, we did have some problems! And when crises arose, it helped us to keep the GOAL in mind instead of focusing on the immediate hurdle.

Let's try to define what we mean by GOAL. A common goal is an objective that requires *combined effort.* A couple working together achieves a specific experience that is unique and valuable because of mutual sacrifice and cooperation.

The word *sacrifice* is not meant to sound moribund. But when two people join together to reach a mutual goal, it's true that each of them truly must compromise his or her own personal interest to some degree.

Gloria: Goals did help us over the hurdles. Some years ago we faced a very big hurdle. We found ourselves overseas without housing or income. Our job had suddenly been terminated, and for all practical purposes we and all our worldly goods were about 27 inches away from the curb.

At that point we did some self-evaluation and goal-setting. Our major goal was to get back to the States, and Dick decided to return to college to earn a degree in education. That required a move from the tropics to a small town in northern Wisconsin. It meant that I became the breadwinner for a full year in a place where there was little opportunity for employment.

We were able to locate a college where Dick could transfer previous college credits and complete his degree requirements in education in one year. I spent that year running a power sewing machine in a sweat shop. That was a far cry from the kind of work I'd been trained for. I enjoyed neither the work, the environment, my boss's roving eyes, nor the salary. But it was important for Dick's career goal and our marriage goal. And that alone made it possible for me to do what I had to do. A sense of higher purpose is liberating.

Dick: There's an often overlooked essential that must accompany goal-setting if you're going to reach your goals. It may seem strange to comment on this—you'd think that when two people make a lifelong commitment to one another, it would be automatically understood—but a couple must *believe* in one another. *Each member must manifest an overt belief and confidence in the other's ability and capacity to achieve.*

How often have you heard one partner putting the other down? A couple may be mystified at their inability to achieve the things that matter to them, all the while engaged in a subtle or not-so-subtle contest of putting each other down.

When Gloria and I experienced our "on the curb" crisis, that was probably the lowest point in our marriage. (I was so down that I'd have had to reach up to scratch a caterpillar's belly.) Gloria expressed confidence in my ability to recover from that set-back and her belief in me has buoyed my confidence and resurrected my belief in myself on many occasions. There's considerable research to indicate that *believing* in an objective is the first and most important step to reaching it.

Gloria: I don't think any goal is ever reached without a willingness to sacrifice. After I had been speaking and traveling for about ten years as a lecturer on personal appearance, Dick and I agreed that I needed a new challenge, a new program. We evaluated my strengths and weaknesses and decided that I should move in the direction of speaking on motivation. Since my standard program involved modeling fashions I had designed and made, with many changes of costume, and Dick had helped carry all that baggage around the country, I think he had a bit of personal interest in that decision!

But we ran into a problem. Dick and I saw my new goal differently. After you live with someone for 25 years you have a pretty good picture of his strengths and weaknesses, and I knew that one of Dick's strengths was the ability to be analytical, creative, and perceptive. I had seen on past occasions that what would probably take me six months to accomplish could be done in one month with Dick's help. So I decided that this time he must again be a few steps ahead of me in the conceptual process. This all helped me to trust Dick, to allow him to lead me into my new future.

Dick invested hundreds of hours to help me develop my new program and get me tracking. At times it was exasperating. When he was on one wavelength and I was on another, the only way we could connect to establish a mutual direction was to debate the issues.

Dick spent his entire vacation consulting with agents and helping with the research, the manuscript preparation, the publicity, and the rest of a seemingly endless list of tasks. The pay-off came almost two years to the day after we had begun, when I gave my new talk to an international convention and received the highest fee in my career. But the fee wasn't nearly as important as *the achievement of the goal we had worked toward.* The sacrifices we had made heightened the satisfaction.

I think the most important part of that project was the belief Dick had in me. He was convinced that I could take my message to the platforms of international conventions. I am sure I could never have realized that goal without his encouragement and support.

Dick: Gloria and I have discovered that working toward a goal is one of the best ways to keep our relationship fresh and stimulating. Striving to reach a goal is actually more exciting than attaining it. Or, as you may have heard before, "Striving is better than arriving!"

Working toward a mutual goal requires that you pool your energies and share your talents. It compels you to tap your personal resources, and thereby also promotes your growth as individuals. It provides the satisfaction and pride of contributing to the welfare of a person that you love and cherish. It gives direction to your marriage.

Identify your goals and you'll strengthen your marriage.

Gloria: I once attended a lecture given by George Reedy, press secretary to Lyndon Johnson. He observed that the women's liberation movement has been the most influential force on American life during the past hundred years.

Undoubtedly the women's movement is a revolutionary force in our society. Some people might prefer pre-liberation customs, but that's an unrealistic desire. Changes are occurring and they are having significant impact on the lives of all of us—women, men, and children.

When we look into the subject of ROLES, there are

three aspects that require our attention. First, we must be willing to *grow;* second, we need to *know* one another in a more complete way; and third, we must be willing to *sow* in the life of our partner. (More about that later.)

Dick: Growing in a relationship means changing. That may be uncomfortable for most of us, and it requires an investment of time and energy. But there's nothing more deadening in a marriage than a member who won't change or grow. When one member remains the same and refuses either to grow or to maintain an open attitude toward new experiences, the relationship becomes strained and falls into conflict.

Growth doesn't always occur in tandem. In fact, we usually grow not as a couple, but as individuals within the union. So it's important that within a marriage there always be support for the growing partner.

Gloria: I recall speaking on this subject to a group of doctors' wives. After the meeting, one of them told me about her personal dilemma. She had returned to college for professional training although her husband was adamantly opposed to her doing so. He refused to support her growing effort on the grounds that his income could provide them with everything they needed. There was a real impasse in their relationship. Her need for personal accomplishment apart from her husband's successes was resulting in serious conflict.

Give your partner room to grow. Recognize how much you have grown during the past year and provide the support your partner will need to become a more interesting and productive person to live with.

After you agree to grow and permit growth in your marriage, you'll discover a need to know more about your partner.

About ten years after we were married, Dick returned to the campus to pursue graduate studies, and we lived in university housing for married couples. At times I felt very uncomfortable. He and his colleagues would sit around rapping over theoretical issues, and I wasn't feeling too intellectual—while I cleaned up dirty diapers or made baby formula.

Then, thank goodness, Dick happened to take a course in psychological testing and used me as one of his practice subjects. Never having felt like much of a scholar, I took the test with some anxiety.

The outcome of that test came to play a big part in my future. To my surprise I scored in the *superior* range in spatial relations! I had special and exceptional ability in this area, and that's where my interests lay, too. That explained my talent and expertise as a designer and seamstress.

What a tremendously liberating experience! I had always thought that I should somehow try to fit into the scholar's role. When I discovered my own gift and valued it as my special talent, it was like finally accepting myself, warts and all! I poured my energies into areas that I was naturally drawn to. I continued to admire Dick's academic interests, but I took no small delight in knowing that he was just *average* in spatial relations!

Dick: The other aspect of ROLES is knowing it's necessary to *sow*. It not only rhymes with *grow* and *know*, but it aptly describes the critical contribution each partner makes to enhance the other's life. Sowing has to do with the respect two people have for each other. That respect is fleshed out through practical, deliberate efforts to help reach each person's identified goals.

I've discovered that the sowing I do in Gloria's life is quite different from the sowing she does in mine. It's not a matter of trying to *match* or *compete* with one another.

She knows I'm a bear for orderliness, punctuality and

similar idiosyncracies. I know she helps me when I'm far less patient and tolerant than she is. I'm aware of how much special effort she makes to enhance my life and make it as convenient, efficient, and pleasant as possible. I continually sense the investment she's making, and I credit her with a large measure of any success I've had in life. Her awareness of the person I want to become and her sensitivity to the times when I feel discouraged help me to accept and learn from the realities of life.

Gloria: Sowing protects the integrity of each partner. If each partner consciously invests in the other's goals, it will prevent the couple from becoming over-occupied with the goals of one member.

Marvella Bayh, wife of U.S. Senator Birch Bayh, wrote about this during the last months of her life. After learning that she had cancer, she had made speaking appearances throughout the country for the National Cancer Foundation. She considered those years to be the best of her life. Not that she resented her investment in her husband's political career, but in pursuing an exalted personal goal she developed new pride in her own accomplishments.

Keep in mind that helping your spouse to attain goals should not stand in the way of serving yourself. The role of *sowing* must be kept in proper balance. Women have been conditioned throughout the centuries to consider their primary responsibility one of giving support to their husbands. I'm glad to see a new day dawning when men accept a part in helping women realize *their* potentials.

Dick: I've got to caution against giving help when it isn't wanted. This is neither helpful nor constructive. You may communicate "You're incapable," instead of "I'm here to help you." Give your spouse just enough help for her to be confident of your interest and support. Leave her with the primary responsibility for getting the job done.

Soul became a popular word in the 60s. That was a period of great social change, and we heard about *soul brothers, soul food,* and *soul music.* It was a useful term to describe a dynamic, heartfelt, or perhaps mystical experience.

Without SOUL the business of building a marriage lacks real impact. You might call it the dynamic, unwavering commitment to the relationship. If there is SOUL in your marriage, there's no doubt about its reality. If it's absent, you and the whole world seem to know it.

Gloria: I think SOUL is *freedom.* Since we're talking about soul, and confession is good for the soul, I'll confess that I had a crazy notion about married life before I got married.

When I was single, I viewed marriage as being the end of the beginning and the beginning of the end. I thought that when I married I would lose my individuality and be trapped by stereotyped roles. I feared having to compromise my own individual sense of purpose. While I respected the role of the homemaker, I saw it as restrictive of my future opportunities.

As I reflect on my perspective at that time, I think it mirrored my mother's experience. She gave up her career in a large city when she married my father, a struggling farmer and rural businessman. It was during the depression era, and my mother's reported hardships left me with foreshortened expectations of what marriage could offer. In retrospect, the only thing that enabled me to make the huge, frightening leap into marriage was Dick's persistent confidence!

Since that time I've discovered the privilege of choosing freedom in a marriage relationship. My own individuality has been nurtured by the love, insight, and balance that a husband provides.

As it says in *Ecclesiastes,* Chapter four: "Two are better than one, because they have a good return for their work: If one falls down, his friend can help him up . . . though one may be overpowered, two can defend themselves. A cord of three strands is not quickly broken."

Dick: SOUL is also *adventure.* Married life must be more than routines, schedules, and monotonous obligations. I have a real need for consistent living patterns, but even I admit that sort of thing can grind you into the ground. Build some adventure into your marriage. Adventure means new experiences and challenges. It means exploring, experimenting, climbing new mountains, sailing new ships, and plowing new ground.

Gloria and I are awed by the adventuresome spirit of some dear friends. He was an executive in a large urban bank and she was involved with clubs and church organizations. When we last visited them they were negotiating the purchase of 40 acres in rural North Carolina. Their goal was to begin a truck gardening operation during their "spare" time. Sherry was going to enroll in some extension courses while her husband investigated the economics of the project. Each of the children also had a well-defined role in the new venture.

We learned their project encountered insurmountable resistance from local authorities. But they're not discouraged. Now they're planning another adventurous pursuit. There's so much soul in that family that you can see it and hear it in their personal vitality!

Adventure is also experiencing failures and successes, laughing and crying, dealing with pain and sorrow, trying and attaining.

Two people who represent soul to its furthest possible limits are Kenny and Carol. About ten years ago, when Kenny was driving home from work in his Volkswagen, he collided with a semi-trailer. His back was broken in seven places. His injuries were so severe that Carol was told it was hopeless. He was unconscious for many months. Doctors recommended institutionalization. They said his brain was so damaged that he had no chance for a normal, productive life.

Carol rejected the suggestions of the experts because she believed in the principle in God's Word—faith that can move mountains: "With men it is impossible, but not with God: for all things are possible with God." *(Mark 10:27)*

She set a goal to do everything in her power to help Kenny recover to live a happy, productive life. She found a job to support them and spent every free moment of her time on his rehabilitation. Kenny remained totally paralyzed for many months. He had no speech, and he was completely dependent on Carol for meeting his basic needs.

Their first means of communicating was simple eye-contact. Kenny sent messages with his eyes and Carol saw his desire to recover.

She spoon-fed him to keep him alive. She drove him thousands of miles to a distant clinic, which was the only one that supported her commitment to Kenny's recovery. She gave untold hours of therapy, with unlimited patience. And she accomplished her goal.

I recently met Kenny at the front door of his shop, one of a few buildings on a small farm in central Wisconsin. He's known throughout the area for his hand-crafted products, and the shop serves as both work station and retail outlet. His handicaps are still very apparent, but he is fulfilled and successful.

Their lives represent a living miracle. Meeting Carol

and Kenny is a life-changing experience. They've conquered every obstacle to reach achievement and happiness.

What do we attribute our happy marriage to? I think the answer can still be best expressed in the spontaneous response I gave those editors in Sardi's Restaurant: "We try to live by the principles of God's Word. They've become the foundation stones of our marriage."

Our successes have outnumbered our failures. We've received more blessings than we've deserved. Through it all married life has offered us rich, unexpected, undeserved, and unparalleled joys—and we've shared them all together.

NICOLE SCHAPIRO

Nicole Schapiro has been called a role model for those who have doubts about being able to find success in the business world. Nicole beat all the well-known odds. An immigrant at age 16, with no money or knowledge of English, she is now a success by anyone's standards.

Nicole is a nationally known lecturer, keynote speaker, seminar leader and management consultant. She has dedicated her life and career to helping people gain the skills and self-confidence necessary to achieve personal and business success. She has published several articles, she has written a newspaper column called "The Best You," and she has also appeared on numerous radio and television programs.

Nicole received a Bachelor's Degree in Psychology

from the University of Chicago and a Master's Degree in Psychology from New York University. She also took advanced course work at Fashion Institute of Technology of New York.

She is president of Sales, Communication, and Image Specialists of Walnut Creek, California, and founder and director of Creative Women Self-Development Institute, also in Walnut Creek. Her companies specialize in training and development and offer motivational programs and individual consultation in the fields of Professional Packaging and Effective Self-Presentation.

As a keynote speaker her most popular topics are: "You, the American Dream—So What Are You Going to Do About It?" "When You Are Afraid, That's Where It All Begins," "Freedom Through Commitment," and "Blueprint for Success."

She currently serves on the board of trustees of the Bay Area United Way, is a member of the Business and Industrial Management faculty of Chabot College, California, is on the board of directors of Equitable of Iowa Insurance Company, California, the Advisory Committee for Evergreen College, and was formerly a board member of San Francisco Women Entrepreneurs. Nicole was recently chosen by the International Institute of the East Bay as the immigrant woman of the year who contributed and achieved the most for her community. Nicole received a Citizen of the Day Award from KABL Radio in San Francisco.

You can contact Nicole Schapiro by writing to 11 Holly Hill Court, Walnut Creek, CA 94596; or telephone (415) 939-5585.

THE AMERICAN DREAM: FREEDOM THROUGH COMMITMENT

by NICOLE SCHAPIRO

Hitler was in power in Europe. "1939 is not the time to have a child," said my father. But my mother believed it *was* time, and I was born, she said, "in spite of all odds."

We were hungry and cold much of the time, and we slept on a dirt floor in bunkers—but my mother believed in our survival.

I remember when four of us shared the one and only orange we had ever seen. I often think of that orange slowly peeled by my mother. I remember wishing I could eat the whole thing myself—it smelled so delicious! But my mother told me, "I can see the day when you will have all the oranges you want."

I remember her words sometimes when I choose oranges in the supermarket. Clean beds, hot showers, central heating, and shoes can also seem the direct result of her assurances: "I can *see* you'll have . . ." We didn't use the words *visualize, plan, believe,* or *goals* in Budapest in the 1950s, but the effect was the same. My mother taught me long ago that the only thing that limits me is my willingness to focus on what I want and to act to get it.

When I was a child I found a wonderful book called *The Book of Wonders.* As soon as I got home from school I would sit down with that picture book. It was about America—the Empire State Building, the Grand Canyon, the Statue of Liberty, redwood trees, coastlines—and my mind and my heart connected with those scenes across thousands of miles! It was in that book that my journey to a free land and a free life began.

My Escape to Freedom

In 1956 the Hungarian Revolution broke out. We heard that the revolutionaries had opened the border and that people could walk out of Hungary. My brother was sick; my mother and father could not go. But it was essential that at least one of us get out of the country.

My parents put me on a train headed for the border and said goodbye to me. We were aware of the great danger in making an escape attempt and knew that we might never see each other again. But if I could only reach the border, there was a chance!

Ten miles from the border the train stopped. The tracks had been blown up. I was taken from the train to the firing squad. As I stood in front of a white picket fence with about 30 other people from the train, a young soldier faced me with his machine gun. He was about 16, like me. Our eyes met, acknowledging for a moment the insanity of my death and his job. I don't remember anything else until I found myself lying in the snow, with the dead all around me. I must have fainted. But I do know that as I stood there waiting for the shots I had been fiercely imagining myself living in America.

I immediately scrambled for cover, and began planning my survival strategy. I had to overcome my terror in order to evaluate my choices. If I moved toward the border I might get caught. But if I did not move, I would never reach freedom. Sitting there, temporarily safe, could gain me nothing, while risking a move forward held perhaps a 50 percent chance of success. That lesson learned in a time of fear and danger has stayed with me all my life. I never forget that in order to gain, I must risk.

I began to follow the train tracks, hiding by day and moving only in darkness. My thoughts of America kept me going. I was going to a place where I would never be hungry, where my children would be free. It was a place where my parents and I could be reunited and live without fear. I moved toward the border cautiously, deliberately, sustained by my commitment. I learned through living it that a simple purpose with focused consciousness is necessary for reaching a goal.

When I was seventeen, I received a college scholarship. In return, I was to speak to clubs, schools, and agencies as a part of a foreign relations team on "Life in a Communist Country"—provided I first learn to speak English! Since I believed my confrontations with death had made me "fearproof," I accepted. And so it started—my life as a teacher and lecturer, and my commitment to wake people from their apathy and make them excited about their possibilities.

As a dinner guest of the Lions Club of Aurora, Illinois, I sat at the head table. While I was eating the first of many hundred "rubber" chicken dinners to follow, I vaguely heard the following introduction: "I would like to welcome our speaker from Hungary, who will share with us what it is like to live in a communist country." It took me a few moments to realize I was on, and by the time I got to the microphone, I almost wished I had died six times over. At any rate, I was positive I would die *right then!*

I struggled to activate my voice without deactivating my mind, and at the same time get the little English I knew going. I also knew that whatever I was to say, I would have to say it with my arms close to my body so all those people wouldn't notice that I was perspiring!

At the mike I looked out at a sea of eager faces. I concentrated on my goal—college education without starving to death—and shakily said, "When I learn how to speak English, and I can, I will return to share my thoughts about life in Hungary. But in the meantime, count your blessings each day for living in this country." I got a standing ovation.

Realizing how truly naive I had been in thinking it would be easy, I made a hasty commitment to become the best speaker I could.

Two years later at the same Lions Club I earned my second standing ovation. My English had improved, but their chicken hadn't.

Success Begins Within

That was a long time ago. Since then I have had to take a hard look at what success and prosperity, both personal and professional, mean to me. My experiences have shown me that in order to attain the success that is freedom we must first define it and then commit to it.

Many people consider me successful because I give so many seminars and speeches, because I am an educated person, because I earn adequate income for my needs, because I receive awards. However, my *personal* definition of success is spelled out by having never consciously gained through other people's loss, having never sold out my personal beliefs for material gains. For the past ten years I have done only work that I love. And I have three smart, healthy, well-adjusted children.

The most important ingredient of my success has been my *personal commitment to achieving my goals.* Coming to the United States from Europe gave me perhaps a wider-than-average perspective. I am aware of responsibilities toward ourselves and others—individual directions affect the collective direction. Years ago I promised myself as part of my goal-setting program that I would read and think every day, listen to one cassette tape, do one positive action for my family, call on one of my clients, write at least half an hour, and take 15 minutes for only me. I am fully aware that each of these actions has some unknown effect on the rest of the world. As we work on our individual worlds, we are part of a process of harmonizing the outside world, fitting together the pieces of a gigantic puzzle. My personal life involves a daily commitment to reach out to others, and my work focuses on helping others to recognize and achieve their goals, finding their success.

Not everyone is ready to make a commitment to a happier, more productive, more satisfying life. But assuming that you want your life to expand for you and the people around you, this chapter may give you a few valuable insights for your own journey to freedom.

Blueprint for Success

I have designed a 15-point "Blueprint for Success." You will recognize some principles that have played major roles in my life.

1. *Clarify your values.* Ask yourself what price you are willing to pay for success.

2. *Believe you can.* Support your case with examples of past successes.

3. *Keep cool in crisis.* Anticipate crises by practicing behavior that will work for you. Do your homework.

4. *Have a plan.* Ask yourself where you want to go, what you need to do, and what you expect to do when you get there.

5. *Welcome change.* It means you are growing.

6. *Focus.* Take one step at a time while watching the end of the road.

7. *Participate.* Don't wait for them to come to you— they won't!

8. *Communicate directly and clearly.* Do not make assumptions. Be assertive and not manipulative. Learn to handle conflicts effectively.

9. *Balance feeling vs. thinking.* Culturally, women have been encouraged to feel, men to think.

10. *Sell yourself.* Learn to build an appropriate image through effective self-packaging. People respond to the way you behave and dress.

11. *Build a support system.* (Mentors, sounding boards, networks.) None of us can do it alone. Create your team.

12. *Manage your time.* We all have 24 hours a day. Never have to say "If only I had the time . . ."

13. *Set limits.* You have a right to say *no* when you know saying *yes* would be detrimental to you or others.

14. *Take risks.* A mistake is only a short cut to knowing how to do it right next time.

15. *Review.* At the end of each day take time to appreciate your accomplishments and learn from your experiences.

I'm going to describe to you the part some of these principles play in my life. One of the shocks I received after I arrived in this country came in learning that there is no such thing as a free lunch! I quickly found out that success breeds both friends and enemies. Along with the rewards there is always the price to pay. It's important to continually reevaluate, to ask "What's this all about?" to make sure that in your life the rewards and the sacrifices are in balance.

I'm talking about value clarification. What you want and what you are willing to pay for it may change at times during your life. Needs change, too, but while wants are negotiable, needs are something you can't compromise on.

When you know what you need and what you want and how much you can pay, you can exercise *conscious choice* over your future.

Take Time to Review

Your success pattern can be a planned event in your life. One part of my "Freedom Through Commitment" program is reviewing my day at the end of each and every day. I sit down every evening and do a reality check of my day. What did I do right? How can I repeat that success next time? I try to feel the sweetness of my successes.

Then I take the opposite tack. I ask myself: What went wrong? How can I avoid doing it that way again? I think about how I could say it, present it, write it, plan it, visualize it differently. I acknowledge how fortunate I am to have this new information. And then *I let it go.*

It's a matter of *conscious competency, unconscious competency, conscious incompetence,* or *unconscious incompetence.* To be successful, you have to know *why* something worked for you. (That's conscious competency.) If you don't know that, you're in the state of unconscious competency, and you are unable to make that success happen again.

Similarly, if you're unconsciously incompetent, you're doomed to make the same errors over and over. But if you figure out *the reason* for the failure (conscious incompetency), you can avoid failure the next time.

This review process makes me feel in control, powerful, and aware that I am responsible and have control of the design of my success, my days, my life. And it costs about half an hour of my time.

Me and My Image

I did not recognize the importance of item Number 10 on my blueprint until much later than many of the others. But now it plays an important role in my life.

I was a college student in psychology in the 1950s. I was an overweight hippie who took showers secretly so as not to ruin my image. My mother came to visit me from Hungary and one of the first things she said to me was "Do you work on looking ugly?"

"Mother," I said, "it doesn't *matter* how I look because I am bright, I have great grades! I'm a terrific friend and a sensitive person!"

She replied: "If you were so sensitive you would realize that nobody will bother to find out how terrific you are because of the way you look!"

Of course it took me a while to recognize what she

was saying. I was, in fact, working at looking ugly, at turning people off, when I could have spent that energy in developing an attractive, positive self-image.

In the early '60s I started to do career counseling with people in transition. I had the privilege of interviewing 300 personnel people and employers to find out what they were looking for during an interview. Some of the most important elements were how the interviewee walked in, the quality of the handshake, and how close the interviewee ventured to the interviewer's desk. Other important elements were grooming, eye-contact, voice quality, and questions asked. It was during the *first 60 seconds* that the interviewers made up their minds as to how seriously they would consider the prospective employee. They made that decision on the basis of the total initial image.

Now a large part of my work involves helping other people to develop a success image. It's amazing what a large part your clothing plays in your self-packaging, and this is the easiest part to change. This is an area in which commitment gets fast results. To begin with, your clothes must seem a part of your skin, not a costume. Many people spend too much money and time on the wrong clothes, and are unaware of the image they project. They want to look thinner, taller, more powerful, older, younger—but they don't know how.

Dress for Success

It's difficult to underestimate the effect of the color of your clothes. Color is a primary determinant of emotional response. Color can stimulate or depress, relax or energize. If you see two people standing side by side wearing red and blue, you will notice the person in red first, but you will remember the person in blue. Red distracts, while blue relaxes and helps people concentrate.

If you are packaging yourself for business success, bright colors are a mistake. Stay with earthtones, neutrals. Create excitement with the use of accessories.

Here are some other steps for successful dressing.

1. *Consider your lifestyle.* What impression do you want to make? On whom? What kind of response do you wish them to make to you?

2. *Assess your body.* Take an honest look at your body-build, your physical assets and liabilities, and learn how to deal with them effectively. Clothes are illusion-makers—they can accent your good qualities and disguise your problem areas. Fashion, color, line, glasses, shoes, fabric are all illusion-makers—shock absorbers for your liabilities.

3. *Consider your feelings.* Which of your present garments are you in love with? Which bring you compliments? Which do you feel the most comfortable in?

4. *Select clothes for a purpose.* Different outfits can make you appear organized, businesslike, sporty, dramatic, or vulnerable. Ask yourself "Does this garment carry the message I wish to send?" Avoid sending confusing, mixed messages.

5. *Watch your posture.* Choosing a garment should take into account the way you use your body. (Have you ever seen someone move by your desk with their clothes apparently two feet behind them?) If you move rapidly, you need a fabric like soft wool that will move with you. If you are more deliberate, you can wear material that is heavier and sturdier, like gabardine.

6. *Coordinate your wardrobe.* Organize the usable garments you have now and purchase what you need to

complete ensembles. Throw out anything that does not work. There should be nothing in your closet for which you must apologize.

Budget is always a consideration when investing in a wardrobe. But remember, you can't afford *not* to look good! Instead of scrimping on clothes, look for ways to buy them more cost-effectively. Don't be a compulsive buyer. Shop only twice a year—don't go "browsing."

Buy early in the season, and buy quality. At the same time, don't be a label or price snob, and don't pay a lot of money for fads. Fads are here today, gone tomorrow, and they mark you as a *follower* rather than a leader.

Many people have great difficulty buying clothes. And it's easy to be discouraged about shopping when you have a whole closet full of unusable clothes that shout "Dummy!" at you every time you open the door.

Here are 15 commandments for a mistake-free shopping trip:

1. Have a "Need List."

2. Know where and why you are going.

3. Have your fingers already done the walking for you?

4. Ask yourself whether a consultant would shop faster and more effectively for less money.

5. Know your best colors and have samples.

6. Keep your wardrobe in two basic colors and accessorize.

7. Have a firm commitment to buy outfits, not one piece only.

8. Shop only in stores with three-way mirrors. You're not only coming but also going.

9. Consider whether the garment projects the image you want.

10. Is the garment comfortable?

11. Do you know how to take care of it?

12. Does it fit the Rule of Three? Can it go to three places in your life? Can you wear it three ways? Does it go with three things you already own?

13. Does it fit your budget?

14. Do you *need* it or do you *want* it?

15. Does it work for you or against you?

I recommend keeping your clothes in tip-top condition at all times. You don't want to have to say "Sorry, I can't right now" for lack of a ready-to-go outfit. Nicole's Emergency Kit for the professional person includes safety pins, folding scissors, masking tape, extra stockings and extra tie for men, a can of hair spray (to remove ink), salt (for wine spills), and an extra pair of shoes. Keeping these things on hand at work or in your car can help make you worry-free.

Does Your Image Fit You?

At times there can be a real difference between the way we see ourselves and the way others see us. I recently gave a seminar on effective self-presentation for a midwestern firm.There were 15 managers in the room and we talked about visual image, clothing selection, and approachability. When we came to the individualized evaluation section—(how we come across to people and what and how we can change), one of the new women managers said: "I feel confused. I'm exhausted trying to convey to my people that I'm open to suggestion, I'm friendly, I'm fun, I'm willing to deal with problems. They still see me as some kind of organized ogre."

As she said this she was standing in front of us in the middle of the room. She was a good-looking woman in her mid-fifties. She wore a well-cut gray wool suit, with both buttons tightly buttoned, a lovely blouse buttoned all the way to the neck, and gray pumps with sensible low heels. Her short hair was perfectly pasted forward on her face. As she spoke, her arms were held rigid next to her sides, her knees were locked. She stood as if responding to a command of the past: "Always stand up straight, dear!"

I walked up to her and asked permission to run my fingers through her hair. I messed it up, opened two buttons on her blouse at the neck, opened her jacket, and added a navy and gray scarf. Then I asked her to relax her knees and elbows.

Finally I gave her a mirror. Her eyes got wide, she smiled a big open smile, nodded her head, and said loudly, "That's me! That's what I want them to see! That's who I've been telling them I am!"

On the East Coast I did another seminar on Creative Selling for an all-male group. One of the men was small in stature and complained that he felt his customers didn't seem to trust him. He said he had to spend a lot of energy convincing them of his honest intentions before he could even introduce his product.

He stood in front of the class in a well-cut pin-stripe suit. He wore black horn-rim glasses that covered his eyes with smoky tinted lenses. He wore a mustache.

Using one of the many eyeglass frames I had with me, I gave him a lighter-colored frame in a larger size to try on. It gave more space for his eyes and there was no tint to hide them. Suddenly he no longer looked "sneaky," or "biddie-eyed," or "untrustworthy," as some of the participants' feedback had suggested.

I recommended that he wear good quality suits in a solid color. Pin-stripe on small men gives the impression of wanting to "look like Dad." It accentuated his small frame, just as his wide tie did. I also suggested he might consider shaving off his mustache. I asked him to consider: How many of his clients had mustaches? How did the people he sold to respond to facial hair? Was the professional price of having a mustache worth it?

I develop hiring procedures for small companies. The clothes choices of applicants and their overall images play an important part in career decisions. I once received a call from a lawyer in Southern California. He said, "I heard you help people package their images. I just became a partner in a law firm in San Francisco, and I need help. Could you take me shopping? I have only one gray suit in my wardrobe—you know we are very casual down here."

I asked him whether he was sure he wanted to give up that lifestyle to become the suited conservative San Francisco attorney, and he replied, "How can I pass up such a fabulous opportunity?"

We went shopping and we bought him the appropriate suits, ties, pens, attaché case, shoes, socks, to create a new image. All the while I was concerned that this was not right for him.

Two months later I met him in San Francisco. He said his head and his back hurt constantly. He couldn't wait to get to his apartment at the end of the day, take off all his downtown clothes, and get into his white pants and loafers. Six months later he sent me a note from Southern California. "Nicole, I feel great! Why don't you come down and visit sometime? P.S. Do you know anyone who can use some good 42-long suits?"

I've given you a lot of ideas on dressing and developing your package, because this is one of my areas of expertise. And the foregoing example points out that however effective your mode of packaging may be in achieving the desired results, it's not right *unless it fits you!*

I Owe It to My Attitude

It's crucial to know yourself. Earlier we discussed the importance of finding your own personal idea of success and deciding how much you want to pay for it. Another aspect of knowing yourself has to do with belief systems.

You have all the qualities you were born with—physical attributes such as eye color and hair color, and less evident attributes such as special talents and emotional makeup. I am often told by clients, "I am *who I am*—there's nothing I can do about that!"

That's wrong. You always have a choice, and part of that comes from understanding yourself, accepting yourself, and believing in yourself. The most powerful resource we have is how and what we say to ourselves about ourselves. It's essential that we *tell ourselves the truth:* We are capable; we are competent; *we can!*

Belief creates actual fact. Again and again I have realized that situations are determined *by my own attitude.* It's my *attitude* which was responsible for my survival and is now responsible for my success. Believe you can and know that you will—for that attitude is your power!

Kathy, a client of mine and a professional manager, was brought up by a mother whose belief system was, "Watch out, everyone will get you—people act solely out of self-interest." So Kathy proceeded to spend all her energy fending off people, worrying about how they might "take her." She didn't find out her mother's belief system was wrong for her until she consciously changed, made a commitment to freedom of thought, and developed her *own* belief system.

The future is only the past entered through another gate—you can choose your own main entrance. We select the door we will go through, the ways in which we put our past experience to use. Your past, your roots, are also your future.

I am thankful for my mother who taught me at such an early age that I could shape my life to my own pattern by wanting to, by committing to it and working for it.

I am thankful for the experiences in Hungary that showed me the truth of these things in survival by my own will.

I am thankful that I escaped to freedom, and for knowing that the real freedom is in knowing who you are and committing to make your life what you want it to be.

BILL MEYER

Bill Meyer, president of Bill Meyer and Associates, a training-consulting firm, has a varied and impressive professional background. A native of the Pacific Northwest, he earned an undergraduate degree in psychology and did graduate work in business administration. He participated in a two-year pilot program in India with the Peace Corps and later served as an officer in the U.S. Navy.

Bill was director of Seattle First National Bank's management development program, was on the staff of Seattle University, and has been Seattle University's varsity golf coach for the past eight years. He is associate editor for *Young Athlete* magazine, a member of the National Speakers Association, and was recognized by the National Chamber of Commerce as one of America's

Outstanding Young Men of 1979.

In response to an ever-increasing public demand for information related to self-understanding and self-development, Bill has developed teaching techniques for increasing personal effectiveness. Once people have a clear understanding of themselves, their attitudes, their abilities, their potential, their goals, and their surroundings, the barriers to happiness and success often disappear. Unfortunately, since these strictly human concerns are not traditionally included in the province of education, the process of personal development is usually left to daily experimentation or chance.

The nationally recognized Bill Meyer Seminars provide a framework of concepts and techniques which enable people to develop more of their own powers to become more effective, more successful, and more fulfilled. As a specialist in personal and professional growth, Bill Meyer has conducted workshops and seminars throughout the United States for groups and individuals in business, industry, administration, education, politics, social work, criminal justice, athletics, women's professions, and family and religious life.

You can contact Bill Meyer by writing to him at 12132 S.E. 15th, Bellevue, WA 98005; or telephoning (206) 746-7646.

PLAY YOUR OWN HANDICAP

by BILL MEYER

Samuel Butler once remarked that life is like playing a violin in public and learning the instrument as one goes along.

John L. Moore, the colorful Kentucky horse breeder, said that life is like entering yourself in the feature race and handicapping yourself as you run.

I like Butler's description because my own violin has been plenty scratchy. And I like John L. Moore's because, as an athlete and coach, I have dealt with handicapping all my life.

The Word Defined

The dictionary gives us several different definitions of

handicap. The classic definition is a physical disadvantage, something that makes achievement difficult.

The dictionary wisely says *difficult,* rather than *impossible,* for Helen Keller became a world-renowned humanitarian in spite of her lack of ability to see, hear, and speak. And Wilma Rudolph won three gold medals in the Olympic Games although she wore leg braces until the age of six. And John Milton wrote the monumental epic poem *Paradise Lost,* though he was blind.

The dictionary also refers to handicap as an *equalizer.* In golf, for instance, players of different abilities sometimes add or subtract points to equalize their chances of winning. We also know about *mental* handicaps that players impose on themselves by allowing themselves to think they can't defeat a better player. On any given day there are probably 500 golfers in America who could beat Tom Watson over 18 holes. If, however, Watson actually showed up at their golf course, how many would tell themselves "No way can I defeat the greatest player on the tour," and thereby mentally handicap themselves into defeat?

In horse-racing, the word *handicap* has yet another meaning. Here, handicapping has evolved into a complicated system—a detailed inventory of each horse's physical characteristics and past performance. By studying these characteristics on the daily racing form, each spectator hopes to predict the relative success—first place, second place, third place, or last—of each horse in the line-up.

The Human Race

Big John Moore likes to think of each of us as a thoroughbred in the race of life—with measurable and predictable potential to win our feature races, whatever they may be.

And he may have a good analogy. If we look at the human "racing form," we soon discover that, throughout history, the happiest, most successful people do seem to share certain attitudes or "habits" of thought. Suppose for a moment that many of these characteristic success attitudes were compiled into a single list or inventory. Suppose that each of us were given the chance to study this list as diligently as a race enthusiast studies his form.

Perhaps, like the wise old handicappers, we could even assign values or points to each category. Wouldn't this help us clarify where we stand in relation to all the "thoroughbreds" who have gone before us? Wouldn't it help us analyze our current strengths and weaknesses? And wouldn't it reveal certain areas that cry for improvement?

Figure Your Own Handicap

The following "racing form" is just such a list. As imperfect as it may be, it will still help you predict how well you are likely to finish in your race. Go ahead. Take John Moore's suggestion: Handicap yourself as you run! There are 100 possible points.

1. Expectations. Give yourself 5 points if you know the difference between wanting something to happen, believing something can happen, and actually expecting it to happen. (Example: I want to lose 20 pounds, I believe I can lose 20 pounds, but do I really *expect* to lose 20 pounds?) Winners *expect* to win.

2. Garbage in/garbage out. Give yourself 4 points if you understand that the subconscious mind works like a faithful tape recorder or computer. If you program good thoughts into the computer, good thoughts come out. If you program garbage into the computer, garbage comes out. Or, as a farmer might say: "Every thought is a seed. If you plant crab apples, don't expect to harvest Golden Delicious."

3. Opinion vs. fact. Give yourself 5 points if you realize that there is a serious difference between opinion and fact. (Example: "It's impossible for a human being to run a mile in less than four minutes." Prior to 1954, that statement was accepted as fact by nearly everyone except Roger Bannister and his coach. When Bannister proved it could be done, dozens of runners repeated the feat within the year.) Remember: Opinions repeated over and over have a tendency to eventually become fact. Be careful of so-called expert opinions (including your own).

4. Your reality vs. mine. Give yourself 4 points if you realize that reality is in the mind of the beholder. Twenty people who observe a car wreck may have 20 different stories of what happened. In the same way, 20 different people who get up in the morning may have 20 different perceptions of what kind of day they're going to have. Reality is often nothing more than the way we've been conditioned to think of things. What's the current reality for you? What kind of home, what kind of income, what kind of life?

5. Habits. Give yourself 4 points if you realize that fully 90 percent of your day may be the result of habit. We get up at the same time, get dressed the same way, drive to work the same way, park in the same spot, meet the same people, and talk about roughly the same things. Are we sleepwalking through life, led by our daily habits? Instead, why not consciously choose and control our lives?

6. Filter system. Give yourself 3 points if you are aware that your mind is equipped with a sophisticated "filter system" that screens out unimportant information.

Do you know that you continually filter everything you perceive, letting in only those things that are currently important to you? You experience life selectively.

Do you realize that your filter is also very good at letting in the kind of information that supports your own opinions? (After you bought your last car, for instance, did you notice as you drove around town how many other smart people suddenly bought cars identical to yours?)

7. Lock on/lock out. Give yourself 3 points if you understand that once you lock on to a particular opinion or point of view, you will have a tendency to lock out conflicting points of view.

Isn't it strange how many people will declare "There's only *one* good restaurant in this town," "There's only *one* good radio station for news," "There's only *one* way to get there from here," "There's only *one* way to solve the problem, only *one* way to succeed"?

There is nothing inherently wrong with locking on to a particular solution or point of view. Understand, however, that once we do lock on, the mind will then have a tendency to overlook or reject new, different, or conflicting information. Be watchful of words like *always, only, forever,* or *never.*

8. Attitudes. Give yourself 6 points if you understand that attitudes are not absolute fixtures in your personality. Rather, they are habits of thinking that are learned over a period of time—and therefore can be changed. We develop attitudes about everything in our lives. We lean either toward or away from every person, place, or thing in our lives. Do you lean toward or away from spinach? Jazz? Baseball? Picasso? Work? Your family?

In a similar way we've developed attitudes about what's possible for us. Can you sing? Can you draw? Are you good at meeting new people? Can you be in the top ten in your profession?

Attitudes are learned. Attitudes are habits. Attitudes can be changed.

9. Words, pictures, and feelings. Give yourself 3 points if you realize that every word you hear triggers a picture in your mind that results in a corresponding emotion. These pictures and feelings can be either supportive or debilitating.

Try these words: *Cancer, death, accident, problem, pressure, failure, can't, won't, impossible.*

Now try these: *Vacation, play, Hawaii, love, exciting, friend, trust, success, happiness, I can, I will.*

Every word, however fleeting, is a seed. When planted in your mind, each seed yields a positive or negative picture, along with a positive or negative feeling. Be vigilant of the words you plant.

10. Self-talk. Give yourself 6 points if you're aware of the silent conversations you hold with yourself. Whether you realize it or not, you are constantly judging and predicting your every action. Do you ever catch yourself saying things like: "I can't remember names," "I'll *never* get it right," "How could I be so stupid?" After a mistake, a loser might say, "There I go again—I always blow it."

Making the same mistake, a winner says, "That's not like me—next time I'll get it right."

Be aware of your self-talk. Monitor the positive and negative conversations you're having with yourself. They could be perpetuating habits of failure or success.

11. Reacting to life. Give yourself 7 points if you practice this simple maxim: "It's not what happens to me that's important; it's how I handle it that counts."

Winners and losers react differently to the same situations. After the great stock market crash of 1929 a few bankrupt businessmen leaped to their death from buildings. Others went on to build new, happy, productive lives. Lesson learned: We may not be able to control the economy; we do, however, have the power to control how we react to it.

12. Dos vs. don'ts. Give yourself 6 points if you recognize that the subconscious mind seldom hears the word *don't.* When we tell ourselves things like "Don't be late," "Don't be nervous," "Don't miss this putt," "Don't forget," we are actually *causing the undesirable to happen.*

Winners continually picture what they *want* to happen, rather than what they don't want to happen. Instead of "Don't be late," try "Be on time." Instead of "Don't be nervous," try "Remain calm." Instead of "Don't fail," try "I will succeed!"

13. Comfort zones. Give yourself 3 points if you understand that the "jitters" are nothing more than a normal reaction to being outside your comfort zone. While Johnny Carson may be at ease on national television, you would probably break out in a cold sweat. On the other hand, Carson would probably experience some amount of discomfort were he unceremoniously thrown into some of your comfort zones. There is a great likelihood that you routinely do at least one thing that would make him uncomfortable.

Understand that our comfort zones can be expanded through gradual acclimatization. We are all doing things today that would have given us the jitters 10 or 15 years ago. (Just imagine what's in store for us tomorrow!)

14. Sure-enuf principle. Give yourself 7 points if you understand that we are continually creating a self-fulfilling prophecy for our lives. This is often referred to as the "sure-enuf" principle. We say things like:

"Our team *always* does poorly in the first half." (Sure-enuf!) "Our sales are *always* down the first week." (Sure-enuf!) "That person *always* bugs me." (Sure-enuf!) "I *always* get nervous in front of a group." (Sure-enuf!)

Remember: As we think, *so we are!* Positive or negative, our present thoughts determine our future.

15. Dreams. Give yourself 6 points if you allow yourself to dream. Recognize that all great ideas, concepts, or inventions sprang from someone's dream, someone's imagination.

Give yourself the right to dream great things for yourself and others. Remove all limitations. Great ships were built to venture out into fantastic uncharted oceans, not stay in the harbor. Thirty years ago Wernher Von Braun could only dream about putting a man on the moon. Gradually, his dream became a goal, and his goal became reality.

16. Goals. Almost everyone is aware that setting goals is the key to great achievement. After all, it's difficult to arrive at your destination if you don't know where you're going. Give yourself 8 points if your goal-setting includes the following:

- Balance. Have you included goals for all areas of your life—not just one or two?

- Priorities. Do you know which goals are most important? Which deserve the most time and energy?

- Specifics. Can you clearly see the desired result? "Being happy" isn't a clear enough goal. You must determine *exactly* what it is that will make you happy.

- Updating. Continually review and update your goals as you go, to insure that they are current.

- Schedule. Unreasonable time restrictions are self-defeating, but do set approximate dates for your accomplishments.

- Writing. Don't just think it; ink it. Write your goals down on paper.

17. Affirmations. Give yourself 6 points if you consciously use daily affirmations to help achieve your goals. Affirmations are carefully selected mental reminders that help keep us on the track to our goals. As you say the words, use your imagination to *see* the desired goal, just as if it had *already* occurred. (Example: "It sure feels great to have lost 10 pounds.")

18. Win/win communications. Give yourself 4 points if you regularly exercise these principles when you communicate with others.

- Are you aware of the other person's "filter system"?

- Do you approach every conflict situation with a positive expectation of a solution?

- Do you express your feelings directly with "I feel" messages?

- Do you ask for the other person's feelings about a situation, and then listen carefully to the answer?

- Do you play back (paraphrase) what you think you heard, instead of simply assuming you got it all right?

- Do you invite solutions that will make it possible for everyone to win?

19. Time-management. Give yourself 5 points if you recognize that "time-management" is "self-management."

- Do you make a daily "to do" list?"

- Do you prioritize this list?

- Do you start and finish your priorities first?

- Do you handle each item once only?

20. Self-esteem. Give yourself 5 points if you believe that the greatest gift we can give to ourselves and others is sound self-esteem.

- Do you daily affirm your self-worth as a unique, valuable and important person?

- Do you accept that you are your own best expert and allow others the same privilege?

- Do you know what your value system is and respect the decisions you base on it?

- Do you affirm your expectations for reaching your goals and bounce back quickly from temporary setbacks?

What's Your Score?

Handicapping can be fun. It gives us the opportunity to see where we are and how we are improving in our feature race. What's your score on the handicapping form? Whatever it is, remember: It's only an indication of where you are *right now*. Identify those areas in which you want to improve and keep on going—a handicap makes achievement more challenging, but never impossible. Whatever it is, you can do it!

As you continue to play over your handicap, remember that success is measured by the peace of mind and satisfaction that comes from knowing you did your very best.

In this game, whether you win, place, or show, real success comes from knowing you are good, wearing it well, and sharing it with others.

JACK H.
GROSSMAN, Ph.D.

A seasoned professor, seminar leader, and consultant, Dr. Grossman has been on the faculty of DePaul University for thirteen years, teaching his practical approach to motivation and interpersonal relations to both graduate and undergraduate students of management. Police officers from all parts of the country have also taken his seminars and courses, which were sponsored by Northwestern University's Traffic Institute.

Aspiring executives and managers have sought Dr. Grossman's services on an individual basis. His down-to-earth, practical, and easy-to-apply methods have helped many people to accomplish their objectives. Because of his active teaching and private consultation schedule, he has limited his in-house seminars to one

Chicago-based, nationally-known corporation.

He is the author of two books, *Achievers Make Things Happen* and *The Business of Living,* which have been used as text in motivation, communication, and personal development courses. He has also written articles that have been published by Dartnell Corporation and various magazines including *Success Unlimited, Industrial Management, Advertising Age, Marketing News,* and *Police Chief.*

You can contact Dr. Grossman by writing to P.O. Box 1008, Northbrook, IL 60062; or telephoning (312) 498-4050.

IT'S JUST UNCOMMON SENSE

by JACK H. GROSSMAN, Ph.D.

To be successful, either in business or at home, you must be able to deal effectively with others. Regardless of your position or station in life, even if you consider yourself independent, the fact remains that you need expertise, cooperation, and emotional support from others.

Despite the importance of interpersonal skills, they are not normally taught in schools. Colleges and universities do not teach us how to be truly successful, only how to earn a living. Isn't it ironic that a country highly sophisticated in technological developments, whose social advancements have provided so many people with the opportunity for a higher education, places a low priority on learning how to get along with others? Admittedly, some progressive companies provide seminars in team-building, communication, and listening. And groups such as the American Management Association offer similar programs for a fee. But compared to the need, these offerings are insignificant.

The fact that interpersonal skills are not normally taught, let alone emphasized, at any educational level explains in part why we are not as skilled in our human relations as we are in our technical abilities. Lacking these skills, many people who are successful by most standards are unhappy and lonely.

Another cause of the interpersonal retardation in our society is the *Me-ism* philosophy that dominated the '70s. Spurred by at least three national bestsellers with underlying themes of "Get what's coming to you," "Stand up for your rights," and "Get the other guy before he gets you," people were given permission to put their own personal desires before all other considerations.

Mind you, I'm all for being good to yourself, for making the most of your experiences, and for not allowing yourself to be used or abused. That's *self-interest.* The difference is that *Me-ism* tends to produce isolated manipulative people. This philosophy tends to encourage insensitivity to others, while developing a keen sensitivity to oneself. Not one of those three bestsellers mentions techniques for getting along with others.

Self-interest, on the other hand, promotes the importance of the individual, but not at the expense of others. In fact, a person can indeed be self-interested while at the same time being considerate and respectful toward others. Self-interested people are able to view others as *allies;* me-ists view them as *adversaries.*

As a professor and seminar leader for most of my professional life, I have been privileged to teach thousands of people how to deal effectively with others by using certain proven interpersonal principles. Regular testimonials from students and seminar participants who have applied these principles confirm my belief that these principles directly contribute to personal and professional success. The typical reaction of my students when they take my class is, "This is just common sense." However, they concede that because these principles are generally not practiced, or ignored, they could more aptly be described as "un-common sense."

I have selected ten of these principles to share with you. I am sufficiently confident of their practical value to make you this promise: By employing these principles you will notice significant changes in people's responses to you. They will be more receptive to you and more willing to extend themselves for you. *You will obtain what you want from others* because you will be creating a relationship that *brings out the best in them.*

Each of the principles I present here is based on the premise that you have no control over how others act or react; you can only control your own responses to what they say or do. This is not to say that you can't *influence* people. Of course you can. But it is fruitless to expend your energies in being critical, angry, and disappointed at others' actions or insensitivity. Likewise, dissipating your energies on wishing or hoping for people to be different also serves no purpose.

The only sensible thing to do is to accept people's behavior as a given and then decide how you will respond. Consider your options and decide on a constructive recourse.

If you are willing to accept this premise, let's move on to a discussion of the principles.

Principle 1:
Respond to Emotions First

When someone directs a statement to you and the message is both rational and emotional in content, always respond to the emotional part first. Respond to the rational part later, after the emotions subside.

Most messages are comprised of two elements. The rational or factual part of the communication is usually conveyed by the actual words. The emotional undertones are transmitted by tone of voice, intonation, and gestures.

Because emotions are irrational and extremely powerful, they tend to cloud, if not overshadow, a person's reasoning ability. If you have ever tried talking rationally to an emotional person you know how frustrating it is. It's like talking to a wall; the person is too preoccupied with weightier concerns to hear you.

There are a number of ways you can respond to a person's emotions. The simplest and most direct way is to make some sympathetic statement that captures the essence of the emotions being expressed: "Sounds like you're upset over the situation," "I guess you've had a rough day," "I get the feeling you're displeased with that decision," or "It sounds like you're really excited about the prospects." Such acknowledgements tell the individual "I'm responsive to the meaning behind your words and I'm willing to listen if you've got more to say on the subject."

Once the feelings are vented, the communications obstacle is removed. By taking a few extra minutes to give others the opportunity to voice their feelings, you are paving the way for your rational statements to be heard. Isn't that what you really want?

Principle 2:
Don't Judge Feelings

Emotional statements should never be judged, since they

are always valid for the person expressing them. Judging that a person should or shouldn't feel a particular way, or does or doesn't have a right to his feelings is negating that individual's uniqueness. It is also implying that there is a wrong or right way of feeling.

Our emotional responses are indeed unique. What may make you angry, upset, or excited may affect someone else completely differently. Just because you may not respond emotionally the same way someone else does does not make that other person wrong and you right. Or vice versa. The fact is that *feelings* are neither wrong nor right; they *just are.*

Therefore, even if you are offended by a person's emotional response, *acknowledge the validity of that response* before offering your own reaction. A simple statement such as "I can appreciate your feelings" will accomplish this. When you respond in this way you are letting others know that you can be trusted and, therefore, allowed entrance into their inner world.

Principle 3:
Criticize Actions, Not People

When you criticize someone, do not generalize. Avoid labels and, above all, do not direct your criticism toward the total person. Rather, *criticize a specific act.* Tell specifically what the person did or did not say or do that disturbed you.

The essence of this principle might best be summarized by the old adage "You can love the sinner but hate the sin." While it is tempting to label people as incompetent, irresponsible, or lazy—to criticize them for *always* doing something you don't like or *never* doing whatever it is you do like—these are all inaccurate, and therefore false, accusations.

The person you are criticizing can usually cite exceptions to such generalizations, to nullify their intended effect. Furthermore, they needlessly anger the person. Rather than gain cooperation, generalized criticism engenders hostility and resistance. People are much more likely to change their behaviors when their *actions* are criticized. That is much less threatening.

Consider how you would react to each of the following sets of criticism: "You are a reckless driver" vs. "Would you please drive a little more slowly;" "You are extremely rude on the phone" vs. "When a customer calls with a complaint, please be more patient and listen rather than cut him or her off so abruptly;" "You never help around the house" vs. "After dinner I'd appreciate your taking the garbage out without my reminding you."

Principle 4:
Accept Criticism

When criticism is directed toward you, resist the natural tendency to defend your behavior. Rather, accept the criticism as being valid from the critic's point of view. Then, if the person is interested, present yours.

When you acknowledge that the criticism is valid from the critic's perceptual sphere, you are not necessarily agreeing. You are merely accepting the fact that differences in perception exist. You are saying that your critic is entitled to his own interpretation. Your attitude will make the person receptive to hearing your views on the issue in question. If, on the other hand, you negate the value of that person's perceptions by criticizing the criticism, you inadvertently risk slamming the door on an effective interchange.

To illustrate how the principle works, suppose your superior said "The marketing plan you put together is not complete; it's full of holes." An appropriate response would be, "OK, what specifically is missing?"

Another example: Suppose you came home from work an hour late and your spouse complained, "You've got no consideration for me. Dinner has been on the table since six o'clock. The least you could have done was call!" An effective response would be, "I know it seems inconsiderate, but would you like to know why I couldn't phone you?"

Principle 5:
Avoid Asking Why

Don't ask questions unless you really want to know the answer. "Why" questions, instead of legitimate requests for information, are often nothing more than set-ups to undermine the other person. If you are not sincere about getting an explanation, *simply tell the person what you want.*

Rather than asking an employee "Why were you late this morning?" and then, when the person starts to explain, interrupting him to say, "I'm not interested in your excuses," be direct. Say "I'd appreciate it if you'd make an effort to come on time."

Rather than asking "Why did you pay so much for this suit?" you might say "Next time you want to buy a suit I'll take you to a place that has nice suits for less money."

Rather than asking "Why were you so disruptive at the meeting?" you could say "Next time I'd appreciate the kind of respect you would want if you were conducting the meeting."

In each of these examples a "why" question would serve to force the person to come up with an excuse or foolish response that would serve no constructive purpose.

Principle 6:
Think Before You React

Before reacting impulsively to another person, ask yourself "What would be gained by saying or doing that?" If the answer is *nothing*, keep quiet until your emotional impulse passes.

Many of us have the tendency to react first and think later, particularly if we are disappointed or angry. Under such conditions we may feel perfectly justified in telling someone off or giving a "piece of our mind." More often than not we react by blurting out the first castigating thought that comes to mind. Then we wind up regretting what we say.

There is a very high price to pay for telling people off. It may make you feel better, but for a momentary good feeling you jeopardize your future relationship with that person.

I'm not suggesting that you disregard your emotions. You can, of course, tell others how you feel about what they say or do. But you can do it in a way that will not destroy your working relationships with them. Control your impulses long enough to allow your brain to function.

Principle 7:
Shun False Pride

Do not allow false pride to sidetrack you from achieving your objectives. When you are wrong or have erred, do you: (a) admit your mistake and apologize, or (b) believing that such an admission is a sign of weakness, say nothing?

When you are confused or uncertain about what to do or how to do something, do you: (a) ask the necessary questions to clear up your problem, or (b) stew about it or keep trying in hopes that the solution will come to you?

When you have an argument with someone who is important to you, do you: (a) take appropriate steps to correct the misunderstanding, or (b) wait for that person to initiate?

If your answers are (b) you may be guilty of false pride. This is totally different from legitimate pride, which is the good feeling you get from doing a good job, gaining recognition for your accomplishments, achieving those goals you set for yourself, and maintaining standards of excellence. Under these conditions you have every right to be proud.

False pride, on the other hand, is exhibited by the person whose actions are dictated by *the need to maintain or perpetuate a favorable image.* This need is so overpowering that it can cause a person to lose sight of what is really important: achieving objectives. I have known people who have ended or seriously injured relationships with those they love, hampered their opportunities for personal growth, and failed to fulfill their commitments—all in the name of false pride. These, it seems to me, are heavy prices to pay for perpetuating an image!

To overcome the problems that false pride creates, you need to ask yourself only one question: *What are my real objectives?* This question will encourage you to consciously consider your priorities. More often than not, you'll opt for tangible and meaningful objectives rather than self-delusions.

Principle 8:
Watch Out for Assumptions!

The kinds of assumptions we make about people influence our actions toward them. If you assume that a particular individual is decent and honest and would not intentionally hurt you, your actions toward that person will reflect these feelings. On the other hand, if you assume that a person is malicious, jealous, selfish, spiteful, or dishonest, chances are you will be on guard and weigh every word you say.

Admittedly we have to make some assumptions about the world we live in and the people we associate with. For example, you go to work every day and perform your job because you assume that you will receive a paycheck at the end of a working period. You also assume that your failure to meet the demands of your job, whether you work at home or travel to your place of employment, will produce unfavorable consequences. Going by past experiences, we are confident that these assumptions are reasonable.

Since assumptions are nothing more than beliefs, speculations, and possibilities, they may or may not prove to be correct. We frequently make false assumptions and act on them as if they were true. Treating assumptions as if they were facts is unfair to others. It can also be embarrassing to you. Regardless of whether a false assumption is positive or negative, when your basic premise proves incorrect, *you are the loser.*

Suppose you purchased some expensive clothes on the strength of a raise you were promised. Consider your dilemma if your actual raise was considerably smaller than you had assumed. You could have avoided the problem caused by this false assumption by waiting to see the actual increase in your paycheck. While it is pleasant to anticipate favorable outcomes, to act on them as if they were reality is foolhardy.

Consider the consequences of my assumption that all my students want is a passing grade. My enthusiasm in the classroom would undoubtedly suffer. Similarly, what if a friend hasn't called you in several weeks and you reason that he's angry with you over some trivial thing and so determine to pay him back by avoidance? You might well destroy a good friendship over nothing.

There are several alternatives to making false positive or false negative assumptions:

1. Verify your assumptions; get the facts.

2. If you are uncertain about another person's actions or reactions, ask.

3. When you must make assumptions about other people's motives, give them the benefit of the doubt. It's more productive to assume that other people's actions are not necessarily directed at you personally, and that other factors, having nothing at all to do with you, influence their actions and decisions.

Principle 9:
Don't Give Hollow Options

Don't give people choices if there is only one response you will accept, or if there is no room for discussion. Rather, tell them at the outset what you desire, prefer, or are able to offer.

Imagine going to a restaurant and being greeted by a friendly waiter who hands you a menu. After careful deliberation, you decide on prime ribs of beef. When you give your order to the waiter he says "Sorry, we're all out of that." Frustrating, isn't it? Particularly if, after reading the description, you developed a keen taste for it.

Similarly, suppose your date asked "Would you like to go to the movies or would you prefer to stay home and watch television?"

You reply "I really was looking forward to going to the movies."

To which your date responds, "Maybe some other time; I'm just too tired to go anywhere."

Under these circumstances you'd have cause to be angry. It's not that you would have minded staying home. But to be given an option when none really exists is insulting. It creates ill feelings. A forthright approach is far more reasonable than leading others on and engendering a false belief that matters are negotiable.

Principle 10:
Respect Other People

All of us want to feel important to the people we care for and the people we work with. You can contribute to that feeling by listening to others and being sensitive to their needs. We all need to feel appreciated; we all need recognition for our efforts; we all need to be accepted for who we are; and we all need to feel that our opinions and beliefs matter.

To develop respect for others, you have to get into their shoes and recognize *their feelings are as important to them as yours are to you.* You don't have to agree with those you respect, nor do you have to share their feelings. Just acknowledge their existence and their human worth.

When you extend respect to others you are in effect assuming that every individual has something worthwhile to convey to you, whether feelings, attitudes, or ideas. You also owe it to yourself to determine whether you can learn something from that person.

Respect is infectious; when you extend it others tend to reciprocate. And when others listen to you, you develop self-confidence and greater respect for yourself, your own thoughts, feelings, and attitudes. The net result is that everyone gains.

Each of these ten principles has been tested many times. If you use them conscientiously you will enjoy relationships as you never have before. Furthermore, by enlisting the cooperation of others, you will increase your opportunities for success.

CHERIE CARTER-SCOTT

Cherie Carter-Scott, the founder of Motivation Management Service, Inc., has provided inspiration to thousands of people seeking their own answers to life's questions.

Cherie holds an Associate of Arts degree from Bradford College and a Bachelor of Arts degree in Theater and Education from the University of Denver. She is an accredited teacher who has taught theater, English, speech, art, and dance.

She has appeared in theater and television productions in New York, has written and directed theater productions, and has trained hundreds of individuals in theater arts and communication skills.

Cherie moved to San Francisco and founded Motivation Management Service, Inc., in 1974. MMS offers 11 separate programs, each based on a consulting process created by Cherie and designed to empower individuals to discover their own choices and direct themselves personally and professionally.

Cherie is currently board chairperson at MMS. She is also a frequent radio and television guest in the San Francisco Bay Area. Her own TV show, *Inner-View*, has included such notable guests as California State Assemblymen Willie Brown and John Vasconcellos; political activist and author Daniel Ellsberg; and Tom Gordon, author of *P.E.T., Parent Effectiveness Training*.

Cherie is the author of *The New Species*, a work that examines the concept of inner knowing and its relevance to contemporary life.

You can reach Cherie Carter-Scott by writing to Motivation Management Service, Inc., 2015 Steiner Street, San Francisco, CA 94115; or telephone (415) 563-3033.

BUILDING
THAT PIONEER SPIRIT

by CHERIE CARTER-SCOTT

What is the essence of the spirit that leads people to the world's great discoveries? Where does it come from? What causes some people to turn their impossible dreams into realities, while others merely imagine?

When Christopher Columbus envisioned a western route to Asia he might have kept his unorthodox dream to himself. Instead he took action to make it a reality. He knew he had to find the means—ships, money, and men—by convincing others of the soundness of a voyage generally believed to be impossible. He made the rounds of requests to the kings of England, France, Spain, and Portugal. His unwillingness to take *no* for an answer finally resulted in the backing he needed to set sail.

Less than 200 years later the first settlers landed in

the New World, a strange, often hostile, land. They and the millions who followed had one thing in common: the desire to build a completely new life regardless of the risks involved. They wanted to escape civil, political, and religious persecution. They wanted freedom and new opportunities for themselves and their families. They believed in their dreams, and they were willing to fight and die for their dreams.

The drive within the hearts of those men and women that allowed them to risk everything for what they believed in was the Pioneer Spirit. That same spirit was the relentless perseverance that moved wagon trains across mountains and the dedication and courage that enabled the bonding together of people with different backgrounds and dissimilar beliefs to form a nation based on freedom and equality.

It's Alive and Well

The Pioneer Spirit is no different in essence today than it was when our great country was founded. It is still alive and well in the hearts of people who make great scientific breakthroughs or realize their dreams, whatever they may be. People with the Pioneer Spirit have common attributes.

Inspired with purpose. People with the Pioneer Spirit are totally focused on their purpose, inspired with purpose. They know what they want and are persistent in pursuing it. They are willing to undergo any hardship, any failure, any disappointment—even moments of absolute despair—without giving up their quest. They initiate their own ever-continuing enthusiasm and drive. They are, in short, relentless.

Willing to take risks. A risk is taking a chance on

something which has no guarantee. True risks contain the possibilities of great reward and great loss, and the element of the unknown introduces fear. Taking risks requires courage.

Courage is always required to move ahead into apparent danger. And risk-takers do this not just once or twice in their lives, but continually. It is necessary to risk again and again in order to make continued gains.

Unreasonable in the face of the impossible. Ordinary people believe only in the possible. They look at the world around them as it is and make every effort to fit into it, to work within its given parameters. *Extraordinary* people visualize not what is possible or probable, but rather what is *impossible*. And by visualizing the impossible, they begin to see it as possible.

New inventions are generally ushered in on a wave of societal consensus that "it can't be done" or "it's impossible." If the commonly accepted belief is that the world is flat, that one can fall off the edge, then it is clearly impossible to sail beyond the horizon and discover a new world.

George Bernard Shaw said, "The reasonable man adapts himself to the conditions that surround him; the unreasonable man persists in adapting surrounding conditions to himself. Therefore, all progress depends on the unreasonable man." To be reasonable is to be powerless.

Willing to be unique and stand alone. Any person who wants to make his dreams real has to sacrifice the need to be liked. Those concerned with "fitting in" forfeit their uniqueness and, hence, their excellence.

Through preoccupation with tailoring their behavior so as not to threaten or offend, they lose their source of dreams to be developed and brought into reality. The willingness to stand alone comes directly from one's self-belief, which must be resolute and total. Self-doubt is an unaffordable luxury.

Willing to push through obstacles. There are always obstacles in the path of materializing a dream. So often people turn back when they encounter the very first obstacle. They may see the obstacle as a "sign" that they should not pursue their objective. Or they may convince themselves that they aren't ready to make it happen, that this isn't the right time. These are all rationalizations. Obstacles need not be deterrents. An obstacle can be a signpost indicating the next step toward achievement of your ultimate goal. It is only a stimulus to your ingenuity to devise a way *under, around, over, or through* that obstacle.

Begin Where You Are

Building the Pioneer Spirit begins with telling yourself the *absolute truth.* How present are these five qualities in your life? To what degree do they motivate your actions? If you don't experience yourself as a person who makes dreams come true, you may find that you are lacking in many of these qualities. You may find that you are strong in several but not in others. History shows that strength *in all five* areas made the "greats."

Are your actions inspired with purpose? Sometimes? Never? How difficult is it for you to take risks? When was the last time you made the impossible happen? Do your dreams collapse like a house of cards at the first raised eyebrow? Do you regularly push through obstacles, or do they turn you aside?

If you rate poorly in Pioneer Spirit you are probably living your life in the comfort zone. Perhaps you have achieved a certain degree of success, and want to maintain the status quo. You play it relatively safe so as not to lose your security. This is perfectly normal. But do not fall into the trap of believing yourself hopeless!

There are many practical and positive things that you can do to consciously develop the qualities that add up to the Pioneer Spirit. Here are some tools, which, like carpenter's tools, will not work unless you pick them up and use them!

1. Visualize what you want. When you find yourself faced with a problem or a situation which looks like it has no solution, create the perfect solution in your mind's eye. Imagine it turning out *exactly as you would like it to.* (You will have to transcend all obstacles to make that happen. You will have to *look beyond* them—ignore them—to see a clear picture of that ideal outcome.)

Athletes imagine themselves winning the race or scoring the touchdown. Business people visualize themselves closing the big deal or signing that ideal contract. Obscure the personalities and ignore all the ramifications and focus on the ideal resolution. Simply ask yourself: "If I could have anything I wanted, what would it be?"

When you come up with the perfect solution, quantify it. Put a date on it—day, month, and year. If appropriate, put a money amount on it. Specify as clearly as you can what it is that you want.

2. Handle the "Yeah, buts . . ." Once you envision the exact result you would like to have, along come the infamous "Yeah, buts." "Yeah, but that isn't going to work because . . .," "Yeah, but you're too old to do that," "Yeah, but she won't like it." The "Yeah, buts" are the reasons you can never have what you want. They are the murderers of inspiration, the nondescript, fuzzy, grey creatures that eat away at your creativity.

What can you do about them? The first thing to do is to *actively notice them.* They can be very subtle, and they usually do their work of undermining you on an undercover basis.

One way to deal with them is to stomp them out when you first recognize their presence. Stand up to them and refuse to allow them to rob you of your vision. A second method is to agree with them. They will go away if you merely agree with them: "Yes, it's true, I probably can't do that—*and I'm going to do it anyway!"*

3. Feed the "I-can" attitude. Obstacles seem to bring out all those "I-can't-do-thats" that ordinarily lie dormant in us.

It's important to program your mind with an "I-can" response to obstacle stimuli. The best way to do this is to put together a list of action steps for overcoming the obstacle. Each step should be simple, clear, and confrontable. You should be able to perform each of them without thinking, without spending time figuring out what you are to do.

The second part of feeding the "I-can" attitude is taken from methods used in training dolphins. When the dolphin jumps over the pole, it gets a fish. When you do something that you said you would do, give yourself a "fish," a reward for having completed the task. If the task was an especially difficult one, give yourself five "fish." Too often we discount our triumphs as insignificant. What good is victory if the reward is little better than defeat? Celebrate your victories! Give yourself positive recognition when you succeed!

4. Propel yourself into "doingness." Many people get bogged down in thinking about a situation. They rerun over and over in their minds what they should have said or should have done. Again and again they anticipate some feared consequences. They make mental lists of pros and cons and weigh the alternatives. When they succeed in figuring out the right strategy, they dismiss it altogether, and the next day *they start from scratch,* replaying the entire scenario from the beginning!

This game is called "Mental Gymnastics." It gives your mind a great workout, but it accomplishes very little apart from the exhaustion you experience from swinging back and forth on the mental trapeze of each issue. The only way to end the game is *to make a choice to act.* Give yourself permission to make a mistake, choose a point of contact, and let go of that trapeze! *Do something!*

5. Rekindle your inspiration. The most common spiritual disease in our society today is negativism. Nothing will suck the creative impulse dry faster than negativism. Whether it comes from yourself or another person, the energy of invalidation is totally destructive to any form of inspiration.

The "brainstorming" process was created to counteract negativism. There are certain rules to brainstorming:

1. All ideas are good ideas.
2. There is no attacking or defending of ideas.
3. Build on each idea.
4. Be only constructive and positive.

Whether you are brainstorming by yourself or with a group, you can create positive thoughts that have the possibility of spiraling into a creative masterpiece. It is only when the onus of making a mistake or saying the wrong thing is removed that creativity can flourish.

6. Free your creativity. Suspending your own critical judgment will free your creativity when you are embarking on a project of your own. Often when a person begins to write a book or a report, for example, his first thought is, "This had better be good!" or, "I've really got to capture the feelings," or "The boss is expecting a lot—I'd better not mess this up!" He begins to feel that he must be brilliant, articulate, humorous, and deeply moving—all at the same time. What this does is put on the pressure and turn off the creativity right from the start. Anxiety takes hold. It becomes impossible to write.

The writer begins to think: "That last piece was a fluke! Everyone will know for sure this time what a failure I am." Under the pressure to perform he feels inadequate, ineffective, small, afraid, intimidated, incapable —and even ashamed.

Setting such an unattainable standard can make a quivering mass of protoplasm out of any talented and capable individual. The solution to this problem is to give yourself absolute permission to write the dumbest book or the stupidest report ever written. Once you've given yourself permission to fail miserably, only success can follow.

The next step is to write or create *whatever is there for you*. Just let your creative sources put words onto the paper unhindered, without stemming the flow in any way. There will be more than enough time to edit and rewrite later.

When this phase has passed, put the piece down for a short while and return to it with a *constructive attitude*. Look at what can be built from what you have done.

Only when the creative process is complete is it time to unleash that critical, judgmental, and analytical part of you and use your discerning eye. To do otherwise is much like trying to drive a car by stepping on the brakes and the accelerator at the same time.

7. *Reinforce the positive.* We are trained and accus-

tomed to thinking mostly about the negative side of things. Your spouse may adore you, you may have just won a three-week trip to Hawaii, your son may be graduating first in his college class, and you may have just closed the biggest deal of your career—but because your best employee resigned you are deflated and depressed. You look at the world as if nothing is going right for you.

When it seems as if nothing is going your way, one thing that will stop that sinking feeling is to make a list of all the good things that have happened lately. (Don't forget to include all the little things such as having paid all your bills this month, that your car is in good running order, and that you and your family are in good health with a roof over your heads and good food to eat.) Focus your attention on *what is*, not on *what isn't*.

An exercise that takes only about five minutes a day can do wonders. Write "Things I Accomplished Today" on the top of one piece of paper and "The Good Things in My Life" at the top of another. Fill each sheet. After you have completed the lists, read them over and absorb them. Then celebrate your assets and your accomplishments.

8. Monitor your own applause meter. Remember the early television beauty pageants and quiz shows, when the audience's applause for each contestant would be measured on an applause meter?

Each one of us has a little applause meter of our very own. It tells us "You did a good job" or "You blew it again." You can control your applause meter if you will begin to notice the things to which it responds. Notice the times when you applaud yourself and the times you do not applaud (or possibly even hiss and boo). Do you applaud yourself for being on time—or do you give yourself criticism for being late? Do you applaud yourself for completing that big project—or are you filled with re-criminations because you should have completed it last week? Give yourself applause for the things that you *do get done,* regardless of the circumstances, and you will see that you can drive your applause meter up at will.

It's important to feed that able and productive part of yourself. How many plants have you seen grow into healthy and beautiful specimens when they are unwa-tered, stepped on, or ignored? Plants need love and nur-turing—sunlight, air, water, and daily care. How can *you* expect to prosper through neglect? Turn up your applause meter and feed your spirit every day. Give yourself the positive recognition that you need and crave!

9. Manage your resources. Everyone has three basic resources at his disposal: time, energy, and money. The truth about all three is that they *go somewhere!* No mat-ter how much money you make, it always seems to dis-appear. You never seem to have enough time for the things you really want to do, and at some point or an-other you always run out of energy.

The question becomes: "What can you do to effec-tively manage your resources in a way best able to give you what you want out of life?"

First, you have to realize that these three resources do not deplete themselves. *You spend them,* whether consciously or unconsciously.

Second, become aware that you have a choice about how you spend these resources. Most people can tell all the reasons why they "had to" use up their resources in this or that particular way. It appears that forces beyond their control are seeping the resources from them with-out permission! Rarely do they admit they had a choice.

Once you fully accept these two premises you can begin to manage your resources. The method involves taking a side trip to fantasyland. Ask yourself, "How would I like to be spending my time?" "What do I want to spend my money on?" "Where do I want to focus my energy?"

Write out a weekly schedule for yourself beginning with Monday and ending with Sunday. Begin each day with the time *you would like* to rise, and end with the time *you want* to go to bed. In between fill in what *you want* to do. Create your ideal week. Then examine it closely to see how it digresses from your typical week. See if there are any ways to incorporate more of your ideal week into your real week. Do the same with your energy and money resources.

10. Direct your energy. Highly motivated people often get so excited and inspired about a project and its possibilities that their vision expands and grows until it assumes enormous proportions. It grows so large that it becomes unmanageable. They then find themselves in a state of paralysis. They sleep, eat, go to the movies, do work around the house that they've been putting off for months, become involved in diversionary tactics of any sort.

A second common occurrence is when there are so many ideas to pursue, so much to eagerly accomplish, so many things that inspire, that a person becomes stymied and does nothing.

Each of these occurrences is a different strain of the same condition: *Overwhelm.* How do you deal with overwhelm? What can you do to unclog a conduit which has jammed on its own flow of energy? Here are some simple solutions.

One immediate help is to remember why the project appealed to you in the first place. What was your initial purpose in doing it? Recall the scope and parameters of the original project and ask yourself if you want the idea to be any bigger than that. Keeping the scope of your idea firmly within your grasp, plan a route to achieving it, building an action plan much like a road map.

Sometimes the ideas come so fast and furiously that you can barely acknowledge them before you are deluged with others, all of which have merit. You soon become confused and uncertain as to where you should begin.

The best thing to do then is to write down all the ideas, making sure to get them all out. Then review the list and select one item to work on purely for the fun of it. Write it as the first goal on a new sheet of paper. On that same sheet, begin writing the action steps you know will need to be taken to achieve that one goal. You can always go back and pick up the other ideas later.

This is the method we discussed earlier: hone down your alternatives, choose, and then take action!

You're Free to Choose

There are few places in the world where people are free to make the choices regarding their own destinies that we have in this country. We enjoy greater freedoms than any other nation on earth. How strange that we so often en-slave ourselves! We shackle ourselves to money, to un-suitable jobs, to imagined limitations, to other people's expectations, to just getting by. We enslave ourselves every time we reinforce our feelings of powerlessness, uselessness, and apathy.

Throw off these self-imposed shackles and allow yourself to stand tall and breathe free! Find the Pioneer Spirit within you and set off to discover new horizons and claim new territories. Like our Founding Fathers, you too can determine your own destiny and make dreams into reality.

EDWARD E. SCANNELL

National Speakers Association member Edward E. Scannell has given more than 1,000 seminars, workshops, and presentations to groups around the country. He is currently Director of the University Conference Bureau at Arizona State University, with which he has been associated since 1964. He has taught at the ASU College of Business Administration and previously at the University of Northern Iowa.

Mr. Scannell has served as a consultant to several companies and is active in professional organizations such as the National Association for Management Education, the International Council for Small Business Management Development, and Meeting Planners International.

He has been on the national board of directors of the American Society for Training and Development since 1974 and was elected to a term as president beginning in 1982.

Mr. Scannell has presented more than 1,000 workshops and seminars to local, state, regional, and national audiences. The author of *Communication for Leadership* and *Human Resource Development: The New Trainers Guide,* he has also written more than 25 articles. His newest book, *Games Trainers Play,* co-authored with John Newstrom, was published in April 1980.

I KNOW YOU THINK
YOU UNDERSTAND
WHAT I MEANT

by EDWARD E. SCANNELL

"I told him how to do it. . . ."
"Can't she do anything right?"
"Doesn't anybody ever listen around here?"

Communication is becoming an increasingly popular term in all phases of business activity. Hardly a day passes that some slip-up, problem, or error is not laid to a "breakdown in communication." That's the popular scapegoat.

Experts tell us that as many as 70 percent of our communications efforts are likely to be misunderstood, misinterpreted, mistaken, misconstrued, missed, or messed. While a .300 batting average is fine for baseball, the game of business demands a much better mark!

If each of us were to offer a definition of communication we might have as many answers as respondents. However it is worded, the essential element of any definition is the concept of *exchanging* thoughts, opinions, meanings. Without a two-way flow there is no real communication.

Have you ever realized how much time we spend communicating? If you think about it, you'll see that we are almost always involved with communication. When we couple the traditional modes of reading, writing, speaking, and listening with the increasingly important field of kinesics or nonverbal communication, it becomes obvious that communication takes place whenever we come into contact with others or the works of others.

Research indicates that many of us spend as much as 80 percent of our waking hours in communication, mostly listening.

Goals of Communication

It might seem unreasonable to expect each of our communication efforts to have an objective. And yet, how often do our attempts to communicate go awry? Effective communication is hampered by lack of objectives. It makes good sense to know what we want that speech, letter, memo, conversation, or phone call to do for us.

To show how often this basic principle is violated, take a few letters from your incoming mail and try to determine what goal, if any, the sender had in mind. You will probably be motivated to improve on the sampling from your mailbox!

Let's consider a few basic goals of communication:

1. To inform
2. To understand
3. To get action
4. To persuade

To inform. What people are not "up" on, they're "down" on! The first goal of communication is to transmit the information necessary to achieve your objectives (or your group or company's objectives). This may be done through words, pictures, symbols, or actions.

To assure understanding. The second goal of communication is closely tied in with the first. It is two-pronged, involving receiving as well as giving understanding. The problem is not so much to achieve understanding as to prevent misunderstanding. The objective is to understand and to be understood.

To get action. Management is often defined as a means of getting things done through others. I suggest that management is the art of getting the *right* things done *correctly* through others! (If your shop is like my shop, there's never enough time to do things right the first time, but there's always time to do it over!)

To persuade. Most of us expend a great deal of effort persuading other people to do things. In one sense, all communication is meant to be persuasive. Each person wants to sell the other on certain ideas, products, or services. It is true that the more effective a person is as a communicator, the more successful he is as a persuader.

Roadblocks to Communication

Why is it that people can't or won't understand? What are the barriers that block clear understanding? Let's look at a few common ones.

Individual perception. It's obvious that people perceive things in different ways. When several people repeat a story, they all tell it differently. Each sees things uniquely. Here is an amusing illustration.

Two military men, a young private and his colonel, were on a train traveling through the Colorado Rockies. They were seated facing two ladies, a young lady and her elderly grandmother. Just as the train entered a long, dark tunnel the lights went out. In the pitch blackness two sounds were heard: the sound of a kiss, followed a moment later by a resounding slap on the face.

The grandmother was certain that the young soldier had kissed her granddaughter and deserved the slap—but why on earth did she slap him so hard?

The granddaughter knew that the private had intended to kiss her. Apparently he had made a mistake in the dark. She had no idea that her grandmother could hit that hard!

The colonel thought: "I suppose that young lady didn't like it when the private kissed her—but by golly, she sure gave *me* a whopper!"

The private was happy as could be: "Gosh, what a wonderful country! Where else but in America could a private kiss the back of his own hand, knock the devil out of the old man, and have no one say a word!"

Inflections. It's not what you say: it's how you say it. Experiment with a simple "Good morning," voicing it as cheery, grudging, and shades in between. Watch the reactions you get.

Read the following statements aloud with emphasis on the italicized words and observe how the meaning changes.

- "*I* didn't say he was a lousy speaker." (Someone else did.)

- "I *didn't* say he was a lousy speaker." (A direct denial.)

- "I didn't *say* he was a lousy speaker." (Although it

was not put into words, the implication is still clear.)

- "I didn't say he *was* a lousy speaker." (He still *is* a lousy speaker.)

- "I didn't say he was a *lousy* speaker." (Just perhaps not a very good one.)

- "I didn't say he was a lousy *speaker*." (Only a lousy boss!)

Impression vs. expression. When we defined communication, we said that it was an exchange of information and understanding. This suggests that communication is for *expressing,* not for *impressing!* Big words may look and sound impressive, but if they don't communicate, don't use them.

Here, by way of illustration, is a classic story. It consists of an exchange of letters between a plumber and an official with the National Bureau of Standards.

Bureau of Standards
Washington, D.C.

Gentlemen:

I have been in the plumbing business for more than 11 years and have found that hydrochloric acid works real fine for cleaning drains. Could you tell me if it's harmless?

Sincerely,
Tom Brown, Plumber

Mr. Tom Brown, Plumber
Yourtown, U.S.A.

Dear Mr. Brown:

The efficacy of hydrochloric acid is indisputable, but

the chlorine residue is incompatible with metallic permanence.

Sincerely,
Bureau of Standards

Bureau of Standards
Washington, D.C.

Gentlemen:

I have your letter of last week and am mightily glad you agree with me on the use of hydrochloric acid.

Sincerely,
Tom Brown, Plumber

Mr. Tom Brown, Plumber
Yourtown, U.S.A.

Dear Mr. Brown:

We wish to advise you that we cannot assume responsibility for the production of toxic and noxious residues with hydrochloric acid. We further suggest you use an alternate procedure.

Sincerely,
Bureau of Standards

Bureau of Standards
Washington, D.C.

Gentlemen:

I have your most recent letter and am happy to find that you still agree with me.

Sincerely,
Tom Brown, Plumber

Mr. Tom Brown, Plumber
Yourtown, U.S.A.

Dear Mr. Brown:

Don't use hydrochloric acid; it eats hell out of the pipes!

Sincerely,
Bureau of Standards

Semantics. Another problem affecting word choice is multiple meanings. Semanticists reveal that each of the 500 most frequently used words in the English language has an average of 28 different meanings. Think of the confusion inherent in that!

The word *round* has more than 70 meanings. The word *fast* may have contradictory definitions. (A fast color is one that won't run; a fast horse runs very well.) In addition, certain words may have strictly localized meanings; beyond the geographical boundaries the meanings are lost. (This is often the case with slang terms.) It's important to make sure that you're speaking the language of the listener.

Inferences. All too often we make assumptions or inferences we later wish we hadn't. Look at the illustration and try reading the message.

Can you see the word *FLY*? It's there, but only about one person in four will see it. (If you're still having trouble, concentrate on the white space instead of the black areas.)

This point is a simple one. At first glance the figure may have communicated what looked like computerized symbols; we may have wrongly inferred that the message was unintelligible.

How many times have wrong actions been taken because "I *thought* you meant . . ."? The lesson here is to take a second—or third—look before you infer!

Emotions. Emotions can be devastating obstacles to good communication. In any person-to-person relationship, emotions play a prominent role. Kept in check, no problems arise. But if one person says the wrong thing, instead of understanding there can be a full-blown argument.

What makes a person fly off the handle? Why do people lose their tempers? The next time you're involved in an argument, review the complete communication exchange after things have cooled off. You'll find that one comment triggered emotions that prompted a quick rebuttal or statement. That, in turn, encouraged another, more pointed response.

Once you recognize that emotions can play havoc in dealing with others, you can minimize the problem. It's important to identify sensitive topics or words (called *red-flag* words) so you won't inadvertently upset another's emotions by using them.

Remember also that emotions play another part in every communications attempt, since emotions that are present are not always expressed. What a person says may not be what that person really means.

And often what the emotions hear is quite different from what the ear hears. For example, "Good job, Smith," may be interpreted by Smith as "Nice job, my foot! What are they trying to get out of me this time?"

Whether you're on the giving or the receiving end of a particular communication, be conscious of the role emotions play.

People. Glance back over the communications barriers we've already listed and you'll quickly see that most of them are people problems. Unquestionably we could list a host of other blocks—like physical distance, distractions, age, or cultural barriers—but most of our communications problems are people-caused and can be people-solved.

How often have you complained "Why can't they see it *my* way?" Empathy—that is, being able to put ourselves in the place of others—is an elusive art. It's difficult to see things from another person's point of view. Having set our minds on seeing things one way, we find it very hard to change our perspective. The expression "My mind is already made up; don't confuse me with the facts" is all too appropriate.

Channels of Communication

We can identify three main types of organizational communication. In almost any organization, communication tends to flow in certain restricted directions. Without a full and free flow of information in many directions, effective communications chains never develop.

Downward communication. This is the most common channel for orders, directives, and memos from top management to all employees. Downward communication is the channel used to explain or teach new policies or procedures. It is also the channel most often *misused!*

A basic problem with downward communication is that in many organizations it is strictly a one-way street.

There is little, if any, provision for feedback. Therefore much of the communication is wasted.

A recent study illustrated just how ineffective downward communication can be. In this project it was discovered that as messages were passed from top to bottom (vice presidents to managers to supervisors), a decided reduction in effectiveness took place at each level. By the time a vice presidential missive reached the production line, only 20 percent of the communication was clearly understood by the recipients. Eighty percent of the communication effort was wasted!

It's easy to see that the fewer the echelons in an organization, the easier it is to communicate effectively.

Upward communication. This channel is too frequently overlooked. Seldom are employees given a chance to bring ideas, suggestions, and comments to their bosses. The result is informal and misleading "grapevines." It makes vastly more sense for a manager to actively seek out the comments and expertise of the people at the lower levels.

Horizontal communication. The strongest channel, and the one used for transmitting and receiving information between people at the same level of responsibility, is *horizontal communication.* It has been conclusively shown that people who work closely have little trouble getting their ideas across to one another. Good lateral communication builds better rapport and understanding among departments, promotes appreciation for the worth of each person, and establishes a cooperative atmosphere.

The Communication Chain

Let's build a model by considering the elements of total communication and looking at each element as one link of a six-link chain. Each link is dependent on the next. The six links are:

1. Sender
2. Idea
3. Information
4. Medium
5. Language
6. Receiver

Sender. The sender is the instigator of the message, the speaker or the writer, who starts the communication process in motion. In some cases senders may not have a clear picture of what they are communicating. If this is the case, there is little hope that the order or message can get through. Communicators must answer these questions if they want to get a message through the chain:

Who? Who am I talking to or writing to?
Who can make this decision?
What? What is my purpose for this message?
What am I trying to say?
What background information should I pass on?
What is the best medium to use?
Why? Why is it important?
Why should they receive the information?
Why is this change being made?
When? When should I tell it?
When will they be ready for this?
How? How should this be communicated?
How can I be sure they will listen?

While these questions may appear to be easy ones, a second glance will indicate they are critically important to communicating well.

Idea. Unless the sender has a clear idea of the message and its purpose, there is little likelihood it can be

189

communicated effectively. One of the most common causes of communication breakdown is the sender who doesn't understand the message.

Information. The communicator must take time to meet the receiver's informational needs. The message can't possibly be effective unless it gives enough facts for proper action.

Medium. For some people, a simple note or a quick conversation will suffice. But others need a show-and-tell and then another show-and-tell after that. It's imperative for us to know which communications medium—phone call, personal visit, note—will be effective in any specific case. There is no one best choice.

Language. Some people like to use big words that are meant to *impress* rather than *express.* These words may look very nice on paper or sound quite eloquent when heard, but if they are not understood they are not performing their task. Your job is to inform, not impress. Never hesitate to choose a short, commonly-used word in place of a five-syllable tongue twister that no one understands.

Receiver. In face-to-face communication, good receivers use not only their ears, but also their eyes. They study the physical expressions and gestures of the speaker. The sender, in turn, must take into consideration many factors affecting the receiver—the receiver's wants, desires, needs, likes, and dislikes will influence how well or poorly a message is delivered.

Listening

How well do you listen?

Have you ever stopped to consider how much you are paid to listen? Of all kinds of communications, we probably spend the most time listening. Studies have shown that people in management often spend 60 percent or more of their communication time listening.

The need for effective listening is not confined to the business environment. Think of the last time you were introduced to someone. Can you recall that person's name? If not, you will likely claim to have a poor memory. But "I forgot" may be only a convenient excuse. Often we never really hear the new name in the first place!

Memory experts tell us that one of the most important reasons for the so-called "poor memory" is lack of listening. The next time you are introduced to someone, *listen first, repeat the name immediately,* and then *use it two or three more times* in conversation.

Poor listening abounds at any social gathering. In two-way person-to-person conversation the person talking often has no audience; the would-be listener is busy thinking of things to say next.

A prime cause of poor listening is the difference in speed between speech and thought. The average rate of speech is 125 to 175 words a minute, whereas the brain can think words at the rate of 500 to 1,000 or, in some cases, 5,000 words a minute. The brain works so fast that the relatively slow word-input leaves time to mentally meander through other things.

The next time you are engaged in conversation, watch your listener. He may be "miles away," tuning you in and out dozens of times in the course of a few minutes. Take that into consideration if you expect the listener to remember what you said.

How to Improve Listening Ability

Although few of us have had instruction in how to listen

well, there are several ways to improve listening ability. One of the most important yet easiest ways of doing this is by simply *wanting* to be a better listener. That's right! Wanting to improve your listening skills makes you pay more attention to the listening process, and that is the first step. Here are some other hints.

Give immediate feedback. Listening without understanding is useless, and the better we understand, the better we remember. Always confirm your understanding by giving rephrased feedback to the speaker. For example, you might say, "What you're saying, Ms. Jones, is . . ."

Conversely, if you are the source of information, ask for feedback from your listener. In checking orders, a simple "Got it?" is insufficient. Too often recipients respond positively when they didn't get it at all. Instead, say "Please repeat those instructions to me so I can be sure I've been clear."

Listen in the speaker's frame of reference. Everything spoken is limited by the speaker's frame of reference. A listener may well have a completely different frame of reference. In order to listen effectively we must get "on the beam" with the speaker and hear things from the same viewpoint.

Watch the emotions. It's easy to stop listening as soon as we hear things we disagree with. We get upset and our ears seem to block out part of the message. It is important to listen harder when you disagree with what is being said.

Listen objectively. Evaluate the speaker and the message. Who is the speaker? What is the message? Many times the unspoken things are just as important as what is said. Always read between the lines.

Watch physical expressions. Many times words are not adequate conveyors of meaning. By watching the speaker's eyes and facial expressions a listener can receive a more complete and accurate message.

Keep cool. Don't get excited too easily. A natural result of being excited is to exaggerate what you've been told. Excitement clouds judgment. When Orson Welles broadcast his *Invasion from Mars* over the radio in 1938, excited listeners failed to hear the intermittent statements warning that it was fictional. People panicked and flooded local police stations with phone calls. In Mt. Vernon, New York, a hopeless invalid was reported to have heard the program, jumped out of bed, and driven off in his car—not to be seen or heard from since.

Be alert. It's an easy thing to let our minds wander while we listen to a story we think we've heard before. We become bored. This happens particularly in cases of over-communication—when a person repeats the same thing again and again. But if we tune out we might miss something new and important.

Nonverbal Communication

One of the fastest growing areas of interest among students of communication has to do with nonverbal communication. Kinesics—or body language, as it is more commonly called—is a fascinating and important field.

It has been well documented that actions speak louder than words. We've all heard people say one thing when they mean something quite different. When we couple all the obstacles we've been discussing with the inherent problems of reading or misreading body language, it's a wonder that any of us can ever hope to communicate effectively or efficiently!

Dozens of books and pamphlets describe all the signals and meanings of our nonverbal gestures, movements, and body language, but the authors do not always agree on their interpretations. Rather than trying to learn long lists of different body movements and corresponding meanings, it might be more instructive and purposeful to simply become aware that *every move talks!*

For example, we've all heard that first impressions are lasting impressions. If this is true, it follows that we should make certain to give positive and favorable first impressions. Recent research clearly points out that it can take less than four minutes for others to form those impressions! The next time you are introduced to someone, think of how important those first few minutes are. Experts in body language tell us that others are "reading" us constantly; the picture we present will turn on—or turn off—our "viewers!"

•

Communications is an increasingly important topic. The amount of time we spend communicating makes it imperative for all of us to continually strive to improve verbally and nonverbally. We can improve our communication "batting average" or level of efficiency by reviewing these basic principles. Then instead of saying "I know you *think* I understand . . ." we will be able to confidently state "We know we *both* understand!"

FRANCES MERITT STERN, Ph.D.

Frances Meritt Stern is a psychologist, college professor, writer, lecturer, and businesswoman. Her books, articles, and speeches have inspired thousands of people to take charge of their lives in a positive, meaningful way. Dr. Stern and her colleagues teach skills of successful, happy living at the Institute for Behavioral Awareness in Springfield, New Jersey.

Dr. Stern says "Success and happiness are yours for the making when you know the recipe."

Dr. Stern's work has been published in both the popular press and in scholarly journals such as the *Journal of the American Society of Bariatric Physicians.* Her self-help articles appear regularly in publications such as *Harper's Bazaar, McCalls, Executive Fitness Newsletter,*

Personal Report for the Executive, and *Training* maga-zine. She is also a frequent guest on radio and television talk shows.

Dr. Stern is a pioneer in the clinical use of mental imagery to help people learn successful living and coping skills. She is co-author of two self-help books, *Stressless Selling, A Guide To Success for Men and Women In Sales* (Prentice Hall, 1980); and *Mind Trips to Help You Lose Weight* (Playboy Press, 1976). Both teach people to im-prove their lives using techniques she has researched and developed.

Dr. Stern provides workshops and presentations on "Stressless Selling," "Stress-Proof Managing," "Organiz-ing Your Personal Strengths," "Coping for Executive Couples," "How to Back a Winner and Be One," and "Building Your Happiness Quotient." She has presented unusual and innovative programs for business and pro-fessional groups, associations, sales congresses, colleges, hospitals, and community groups throughout the United States and Canada.

Dr. Stern earned a doctorate from New York Univer-sity in 1972 and has had additional training at Temple University School of Medicine, Department of Psychia-try. She is a member of the American Psychological As-sociation, the New Jersey Public Health Association, the American Society for Training and Development, and the Association for the Advancement of Behavior Therapy. She is a member of the Executive Board of the American Society for the Study of Mental Imagery.

You may contact Frances Meritt Stern by writing to the Institute for Behavioral Awareness, 810 South Spring-field Avenue, Springfield, NJ 07081; or telephone (201) 376-8744.

STRESS AND HOW TO COPE WITH IT

by FRANCES MERITT STERN, Ph.D.

Stress is as American as apple pie; all of us experience stress as part of our existence. It can be positive and constructive, such as the mobilizing, energizing tension experienced by an athlete before competing or by a speaker facing an audience. It can also be as negative and debilitating as a sudden skid on a patch of ice or a nasty put-down by a friend.

Sometimes stress leads us to experience strain and tension that is short-lived. That kind of stress is a valuable friend—if it is positive it adds excitement, pleasure, and spice to our lives; it stretches our tolerance for tension. At other times the stress we experience is more severe. It may build slowly and seem to go on forever. Then stress becomes negative and an enemy.

Stress of this sort can disrupt our ability to concentrate, be creative, problem-solve, eat, sleep, laugh, love, and generally enjoy life. Unfortunately, this happens to most of us some time in our lives. If this kind of stress occurs frequently, pervades many areas of our lives, and is strong enough, the disruption becomes severe. It negatively affects our minds, our bodies, and our relationships with others.

Let's try to define what we mean by *stress*. A textbook definition might include wear-and-tear of everyday life, strain and tension, and pressure capable of throwing one's system out of balance. The most obvious stress is physical, but the word applies equally to mental anxiety or bodily arousal.

Psychological Stress

Psychological or emotional stress is often intangible. We experience it but can only evaluate it indirectly. When you break a leg you usually know how it happened. You can feel the pain and see the bruise. It's possible to look at X-rays, locate the break, set the leg in a cast, and go through a healing process. It's easy to discern when and to what extent the injury has healed.

Psychological stress, on the other hand, does not fit this "get sick and get well" model. We cannot measure it precisely, picture it easily, or even cure it. Indeed, we don't *want* to cure it, if that means eliminating emotional stress altogether. We all need some stress in our lives to motivate and energize us. How much stress each of us can tolerate, however, is a personal issue.

How much stress we feel and how much we can handle is based on our perception of things. Whereas one person may be delighted at the job change which moves him across the country, another person may be devastated by the thought of such a move and anxiously seek alternative employment.

Likewise, emotional arousal that you may perceive as pleasurable may be stressful and upsetting to someone else. For example, a business trip to a southern island might be your dream come true: a paid opportunity to combine work with pleasure. However, if you were sun-sensitive and did not tolerate heat well, you wouldn't look forward to that trip at all. Stress varies with the individual.

Stress can be either a friend or an enemy. Do you work harder when you have a deadline to meet? Do you enjoy the challenge of competitive sports? If your answer is *yes*, then stress is working for you. However, if you work day and night, seldom relax, and always worry about losing, then stress is working against you and needs to be managed more effectively.

Symptoms of Stress

The symptoms of excessive stress can vary. Headaches, fatigue, indigestion, irregular heartbeat, irritability, and diarrhea can all be symptoms of any number of diseases. These same complaints can also indicate stress overload. When physiological symptoms mask stress they often are treated as organic diseases with poor results—the treatment does not relieve the symptoms and the stress is not reduced. Nevertheless, it always makes sense to check out such symptoms with a physician.

Many illnesses are stress-related. That is not to say that stress *causes* the disease; but stress often does play a major role in precipitating it or increasing its severity.

Some illnesses that have been identified as possibly stress-related are hypertension, coronary failure, obesity, alcoholism, ulcers, kidney malfunction, headache, back pain, allergy, colitis, and skin acne. These are high prices to pay for unmanaged—often unrecognized and undiagnosed—stress.

Stress-Inducing Thoughts

Stress involves an important personal component. How high we aim and how much we demand of ourselves contributes to both physical and psychological stress. Our perception of events, interpretation of situations, and understanding of options also play a major role in how much tension we experience and how we handle it.

What you *say to yourself* influences what you do and how you feel. If you should miss out on a job opportunity you might tell yourself that you are rejected, unworthy, and incompetent. You would then probably sulk, feel despondent, and give up for a while. However, if you accepted that out of the many applicants another person may well have had superior qualifications, you would then be likely to take what you learned, improve your chances, and forge ahead.

Stress in the first instance is considerable, in the second negligible. If stress-inducing thoughts do you in, you can learn to restructure them to curb the negative stress.

Coping Behaviors

The ways in which we react to stress can either increase it or reduce it. We all have our own ways of dealing with stress. There are many different coping responses. Some of these work for us effectively; others work against us. Inappropriate coping responses are not only ineffectual but also perpetuate stress. Do you recognize any of your coping behaviors here?

crying	exercising
yelling	smoking
sleeping	nail-biting
worrying	making lists
problem-solving	deep-breathing
taking time out	drinking
eating	scrubbing the floor

Which of these behaviors would work for you? Which would work against you?

Sometimes stress is defined in terms of the number of tension-producing events one has had in a given time period. However, the greatest harm comes from negative "creeping stress," or stress build-up. Getting a divorce or changing your job is stressful. However, you are more likely to fall victim to a full-blown stress attack if you stay in a bad marriage for 20 years or work at a job you hate day after day. Pervasive stress requires daily care.

Stress can originate from within yourself, out of your own fears, apprehensions, and uncertainties. Stress can come from others, by way of demands, expectations, or imposed requirements. Stress can also be generated by situations, such as encountering an unexpected detour, being party to an argument, or getting married. In any case, however, *you* determine the intensity and severity of your response.

The specific event or accumulation of events that triggers a stress response is called a *stressor* or *cue*. Stressors or cues can be happy or sad, good or bad. The birth of a child triggers stress just as the loss of a loved one does. Your body responds to any stress without differentiating between positive and negative events.

Stressors are perceived and evaluated by you. An

event is a potential stressor, a cue capable of eliciting a response. Whether or not we actually do respond depends on our own perception, thoughts, and previous experience with similar cues. That explains why people react differently to the same cue. If we do react, our responses are manifested in three areas we've already discussed: our thoughts, our bodies, and our actions. Stress responses in all these areas perpetuate themselves and become cyclical. That is, if you feel a skipped heartbeat and sweaty palms, you may begin to worry and become irritable. This irritability leads to lessened productivity, which may increase the tension. Then you become fatigued and develop a headache. This causes additional anxiety. The cycle is now well in motion.

Breaking the Cycle

How can you break this cycle and make stress work for you? Here's where stress-management strategies come in.

Let's take a closer look at what happens to our bodies in stressful situations. Hans Selye, the "father of stress management," described the fight/flight response with which our bodies respond. In the face of perceived stress, your body automatically tenses up and mobilizes for action. This is like automatically switching *on*. When the danger subsides and the stress is resolved, your body relaxes and switches *off*. But what happens when you face continued uncertainty with no-exit problems? The system never really shuts off—it smolders. This can lead to serious physical and emotional consequences.

Coping strategies can influence this switch and put you back in control. Here is a sort of first-aid kit for bringing yourself down when you are highly stressed.

1. *Deep-breathe to calm your body.* When you are

aroused and have physiological manifestations of stress—from sweaty palms to a migraine headache—inhale slowly through your nose and fill your chest with air. Hold it for a count of seven, then exhale slowly through your mouth. Feel your whole body relax. Repeat this three times or more until you feel calmer.

2. *Take a mind trip.* Mental imagery is especially useful in stress management because your body can scarcely tell imagined images from reality. You can develop vivid mental pictures to view whenever you wish. Your mind, like your body, cannot be in two places at once—so projecting positive imagery on your inner movie screen will produce a significant drop in your tension level on stressful occasions.

Think of a favorite place—one you have been to or would like to visit. Get the picture firmly in mind. What is the scenery like? What are the colors, sounds, smells, and tastes? Use all of your senses to make the scene as vivid as possible, then put yourself into the scene.

Use this favorite place as a mini-vacation, a time-out from stress. Use it to reward yourself for a job well done. It will give both your mind and your body a chance to relax.

3. *Blow the whistle on worry.* Why do we worry? If you worry about a problem and reach a solution, then the worrying has been productive. But if the worry goes nowhere and produces thoughts or images that go cycling on and on in your mind, into all sorts of catastrophes, that is counter-productive and stress-producing.

What can you do when your worries get out of control? First, keep a log of your worries—when you worry, what you worry about, where you worry, and where in your body you feel the tension. Sit down wherever a lot of your worrying takes place and make yourself think about whatever is really bothering you. Then blow a whistle, clap your hands or snap your fingers. The objective is for the noise to interrupt your catastrophizing.

Every time the worry cycle starts, *make this noise.* If you are in a situation where the sound would be inappropriate, image the noise. Picture yourself blowing a whistle, for example. Hear the sound. Say *stop!*

With practice, you'll eventually be able to hear the whistle in your head without using any outward sign. Then, when you've succeeded at stopping the worry, take a mind trip to your favorite place.

4. *Tell yourself what to think.* Suppose you are going to give an important speech or sales presentation. Your worrisome thoughts tend to increase the tension and the possibility of performing poorly, since thoughts often guide actions and function as a self-fulfilling prophecy.

Thus, *what you think is what you do.* It's like having an internal coach calling out the plays.

Inner self-instructions that are negative and defeating can result in increased stress and decreased performance. Positive self-instructions tend to increase the ability to cope and decrease the tension.

Stop the negative self-instruction and then use internal coaching to replace the vanquished thoughts with positive ones.

For example, in making a public presentation you would probably go through four stress stages. When preparing for your speech, consider these phrases:

- "Don't worry; just concentrate on what has to be done."
- "I can develop a strategy to deal with this."
- "I can prepare myself by focusing on my stress-management skills."

When actually making the speech, say to yourself:

- "One step at a time. I can handle it that way."
- "Stay focused."
- "Just let me concentrate on what I'm doing and saying."
- "This tension is OK. It can psych me up to meet the challenge."
- "I can use one of my coping skills."

Sometimes there is a point at which the tension is almost overwhelming. This is the time to instruct yourself:

- "Just pause. I can hold on."
- "My stress will come down if I allow it to."
- "I need to control the fear, not eliminate it."
- "I'll keep focused on my presentation. That will help me through."
- "Relax. Take a deep breath."

After you have successfully managed the stress, you might tell yourself:

- "It worked—I didn't get so uptight this time."
- "When I control my ideas I control the stress."
- "Boy it feels good to be less tense!"

Make your new positive self-instructions short, clear, specific, and direct.

Put It to Work

This first-aid kit for stress will help you to lower your stress to a manageable level and raise your tolerance level too. This means an increased ability to handle tension.

To sum up: When a stress attack hits you, *deep breathe* your body down and put psychological distance between you and the stressors by taking a mental *time-out*. When you are more relaxed, *blow the whistle* on the negatives and fill the spaces in your mind with positives from your self-coaching instructions. Remember:

- Stress is inescapable, personal, and affects your body, thoughts, feelings, and actions.

- Stress can be positive or negative. It can be triggered by yourself, by others, or by situations.

- Stress is also cyclical, and our coping responses to stress-inducing events are learned.

- Finally, stress needs to be dealt with on a daily basis. By doing so, it becomes easier to manage.

These techniques are portable and easy to use; carry your first-aid kit with you. Try at least one of these techniques, master it, and build it into your life. The life you save may be your own!

HOWARD W. BONNELL

Howard Bonnell began his career in sales with World Book-Childcraft International, Inc. in 1938. He rose rapidly through the managerial ranks to the highest level of field management, branch manager.

In 1942 Mr. Bonnell entered the Air Force. He served as a pilot for four years, returning to World Book-Childcraft in 1946.

In 1955 he was brought into the home office in Chicago as the company's first zone manager of the Canadian operation. In 1963 he was promoted to vice president. In 1964 he was appointed zone sales manager of the western third of the United States.

His appointment as director of sales training for the United States and Canada came in 1972. He presently holds the position of vice president and director of sales management development.

Mr. Bonnell was the creator of the company's Sales Management Development Program structured to develop the highest level of management. This program is unique in the industry. He has created numerous other sales and sales management programs for World Book-Childcraft and conducts sales and sales management seminars for the company in Australia, England, Ireland, Scotland, France, and South Africa.

In 1973 Mr. Bonnell began to give talks and seminars outside the company. His first engagement was with the Nightingale-Conant Human Resources Congress in Chicago. Since then he has been engaged by such clients as IBM of Canada, Canadian Life, Metropolitan Life, Century 21, Filter Queen, Illinois Bell Telephone, Farmers Insurance Group, Beckley-Cardy Company, Culligan Soft Water, American Marketing Association, and PMA Rally in Chicago.

His book, *Give Yourself a Raise in Direct Selling,* has been published by Frederick Fell. He is now writing another book on sales management and plans soon to devote himself full-time to the speaking circuit.

You can contact Howard Bonnell by writing to P.O. Box 3855, Merchandise Mart Plaza, Chicago, IL 60654; or telephone (312) 245-3412 or (312) 251-6489 (evenings).

THE HAZARDS OF AVERAGE THINKING

by HOWARD W. BONNELL

Much has been said and written about what it takes to be an achiever, to rise above mediocrity. Dr. David Schwartz, in his book *The Magic of Self Direction*, states that eighty percent of everything good—happiness, love, money, peace of mind—is owned by twenty percent or less of the population. Sales records show that eighty percent of all sales are made by twenty percent of the sales force.

My 42 years' experience in recruiting and managing salespeople has given me an excellent laboratory to study both the achievers and the non-achievers. Most of the people I recruited had never sold before, and most of them were in the eighty-percent group, non-achievers.

It is important to understand that the difference between the eighty-percenters and the twenty-percenters is not intelligence, luck, or talent. Both begin life with equal potential. The difference is *acquired*, and it is one of philosophy. The question is, what shapes the thinking of the eighty-percenters, as opposed to the achievers?

Eighty-Percent Parents

Parents are one of the most important factors in the shaping of any person's philosophy. Naturally, the chance of having parents who are eighty-percenters is four times greater than that of having twenty-percent parents.

Psychologists agree that more than three-quarters of an individual's adult intelligence is established during the first four years of life. This is the period during which the ego is being shaped along the lines of the parents' life pattern. The eighty-percent philosophy would include the following: Take no risks, set no goals. Just take life as it comes to you, and don't try to be or do anything special. Don't expect to like what you do—just hang in there and do your job.

Children of eighty-percenters may hear from time to time that people who achieve are *lucky*, or *dishonest*. They are taught that the only way to get ahead is by taking advantage of other people. They learn that their goal in life is to get security. This usually involves a job with little responsibility and few challenges. They are never told that security comes from within.

Formal training. This early exposure to their parents' philosophy is reinforced when children go to school. Fortunate is the child who is taught by a twenty-percent teacher, but so greatly in the majority are the non-achievers in education, as everywhere else, that the preponderance of his instruction will come from the eighty-percenters.

Peer conditioning. When the school years are over and these young adults venture forth to look for jobs, their eighty-percent friends (who may well outnumber the achievers by four-to-one) encourage them to get a no-risk job that provides security. This is an easy route to choose when one is just starting out; self-esteem is generally poor and approval from others is very important. (An eighty-percenter needs the approval of other people as a substitute for self-acceptance.)

The goal, then, is a job that pays a living wage—one that results in the usual raises and pays the bills with a little extra for amenities.

Excuses. People become what they are conditioned to be, and so long as eighty-percenters allow themselves to be influenced by other eighty-percenters, they will be controlled by the philosophy of failure. Of course when this happens, they blame their employers, the government, bad luck, or lack of formal education.

Certainly the lack of a formal education closes some doors to opportunity in this modern world, but it doesn't close *all* doors. I know a young man with an eighth-grade education who began his sales career by selling *World Book Encyclopedia* part-time. Now he is a branch manager, owns a fine home and a condominium in Hawaii, and grosses more than $100,000 per year. He, too, could have used lack of formal education as an excuse, but he didn't. The company offered him an opportunity, not a job, and he took it.

Can They Change?

Eighty-percenters have little chance of getting into the twenty-percent group unless they change their philosophy and their thought patterns. These people are rarely exposed to the success psychology. They haven't read Napoleon Hill's book *Think and Grow Rich,* or Zig Ziglar's book *See You at the Top,* or any of Norman Vincent Peale's books.

These people never heard great speakers spell out the rules of success. They have had little or no contact with twenty-percenters. And until they do, until they encounter the success message, they will probably remain where they are, in the eighty-percent group.

The average thinker is not aware of the subconscious mind and how it controls us. There are people driving buses, delivering milk, working at airline counters, and hostessing in restaurants who have the potential for high achievement, but they will never join the twenty-percent group until they hear and accept a message of hope, inspiration, and positive thinking.

The Formula for Success

Robert Collier, in his book *The Secret of the Ages,* says: "You may have anything you want provided that you

1. know exactly what you want
2. want it badly enough
3. confidently expect to attain it
4. persistently determine to obtain it, and
5. are willing to pay the price of its attainment."

The average thinker has never heard of this formula. (And even if he did he would not believe that it applied to him!) Let's examine these five provisions and see how the eighty-percenter would visualize them.

Know exactly what you want. In the first place, the average person has no goals. What then does he want? In most instances he wants to eventually pay for a home, to buy a new car every three or four years, to take a little vacation once a year, and to take his family to the movies once a week. He has no plans beyond these immediate needs. He can't sustain an interest in long-range goals.

Until a person knows what he wants there can be little achievement. There is a good reason why more people have graduated from the eighty-percent group to the twenty-percent group in sales than in any other profession. When a person enters sales, his manager may be the first person in his entire life to have ever suggested goals. If the manager understands how to help the person establish goals, it becomes a life-changing experience.

Want it badly enough. Most people have wants. They want to be more popular, earn more money, have more conveniences, or live in a more prestigious neighborhood.

A friend from the Air Force lived in the same city I did. He frequently told me, "I wish I had the kind of job you have." He had the talent to achieve what I was achieving, but he chose to envy me instead.

Envy should not be mistaken for ambition. His job permitted him a day off each week, and he played golf nearly every week. He didn't want to sacrifice his day off to gain a more productive life. He enjoyed what behavioral scientists call the "comfort zone."

In all probability, most eighty-percenters will never want something badly enough to get it unless someone else enters the picture to constantly reinforce the want and keep them committed.

Confidently expect to get it. Even though a goal has been established, the average thinker has little faith that it will be reached. And lack of confidence, in turn, diminishes the probability of its attainment. Low confidence equals low commitment. (The sales manager, again, plays an important role here by providing assurance and encouragement.) The first goal should be obtainable in a reasonably short time to take into account the eighty-percenter's difficulty in sustaining high interest over a longer period.

It is good to remember that the average thinker opts for immediate gain and long-range loss. The young person who quits school to get a job so he can buy a car and get married has elected to go for immediate gain, forfeiting the almost certain long-range gain of staying in school. The adult who goes to a movie instead of reading a self-improvement book has done the same thing.

Persistently determine to attain it. The average thinker has not developed persistence and perseverance. Without encouragement from his supervisor or manager there is great likelihood that he will give up. The eighty-percenter needs constant reinforcement from somebody he respects and has confidence in.

When I was a sales manager in the field, I would make an appointment with a new representative to work together making sales calls. The representative would often call me the evening before to say that something had come up and he couldn't work the next day.

What had come up were the butterflies in his stomach. The reluctance to face fears becomes a habit, and each time those representatives "copped out" they became weaker and put more tarnish on their self-esteem.

I was often successful in getting a representative to face his fears, and each time he did he liked himself better. In most instances, however, he would not have persisted without my help.

Are willing to pay the price. Unless the first four provisions are strong the average person will not pay the price. While we often hear about the price one must pay for success, rarely is the price of mediocrity mentioned. Mediocre people pay a price too—the greatest price of all is low self-esteem. It is not even possible to enjoy the fruits of high achievement when one has low self-esteem.

Faith in Things Unseen

For the eighty-percenter, changing philosophies is a process of evolution rather than revolution. The change is gradual, and largely unseen. The average thinkers have little faith in things unseen. They follow the crowd. In our company, when we recruit a new person into one of our organizations we try to isolate that individual from the average performers.

The eighty-percenter hasn't read what John M. Thomas said: "Keep out of the undertow caused by those who drift backwards. You must regulate your life by the standards you admire when you are at your best."

Or what Mark Twain said: "We are discrete sheep; we wait to see how the drove is going, and then go with the drove. We have two opinions; one private, which we are afraid to express; and another we force ourselves to wear to please Mrs. Grundy, until habit makes us comfortable in it, and the custom of defending it presently makes us love it, adore it, and forget how pitifully we came by it."

If the average thinker is managed properly by someone who indicates confidence in him, and he reaches the first short-range goal, it is a meaningful victory. It becomes a winning situation and his self-esteem has taken on a new luster. The establishment of a new goal then is crucial, and the average thinker has more confidence in reaching the next goal than he did the first goal.

To step out of the crowd represents risk—fear of failure and losing comes to the fore. This may be the main obstacle to achievement for the average thinker. The remedy for this is periodical success feedback. Herbert Kaufman said: "Failure is only postponed success so long as courage coaches ambition. The habit of persistence is the habit of victory."

And Then What?

Once a person has broken through the barriers that initially stand between him and success, how does he sustain his new positive philosophy? I recommend the words of some of our greatest achievers and individualists. They are a never-failing source of inspiration and support.

- *Thomas Edison:* Restlessness is discontent—and discontent is the first necessity of progress. Show me a thoroughly satisfied man and I will show you a failure.

- *Gilbert Arland:* When an archer misses the mark he turns and looks for the fault within himself. Failure to hit the bull's-eye is never the fault of the target! To improve your aim, *improve yourself.*

- *Napoleon Hill:* The only limitations of the mind are the ones it is willing to accept.

- *Sidney J. Harris:* Ninety percent of the world's woe comes from people not knowing themselves, their abilities, their frailties, and even their real virtues. Most of us go almost all the way through life as complete strangers to ourselves—so how can we know anyone else?

- *Charles Kettering:* It is amazing what ordinary people can do if they set out without preconceived notions.

- *Cardinal Gibbons:* The higher men climb the longer

their working day. And any young man with a streak of idleness in him may better make up his mind at the beginning that mediocrity will be his lot. Without immense, sustained effort he will not climb high. And even though fortune or chance were to leave him high, he would not stay there. For to stay at the top is almost harder than to get there. There are not office hours for leaders.

- *Thomas Mann:* But self-examination, if it is thorough enough, is nearly always the first step towards change—no one who learns to know himself remains just what he was before.

Continuing on the Path

Average thinkers try to avoid difficulties because they see them as blocks to success. They don't understand that difficulties are *stepping stones* to success. Major John L. Griffith said: "I do not want anybody to convince my son that someone will guarantee him a living. I want him rather to realize that there is plenty of opportunity in this country for him to achieve success, but whether he wins or loses depends entirely on his own character, perseverance, thrift, intelligence, and capacity for hard work."

So many people want to get, but not give. Albert Schweitzer provided our society with an unsurpassed model for giving. He said "I don't know what your destiny will be, but one thing I know; the only ones among you who will be really happy are those who will have sought and found how to serve."

In order to continue on the path of achievement, it's necessary to learn from others. Someone once said: "Any fool can learn from experience, but it takes a wise man to learn from others."

Joseph Marshall Wade said: "If I wanted to become a tramp, I would seek information and advice from the most successful tramp I could find. If I wanted to become a failure I would seek advice from men who have never succeeded. If I wanted to succeed in all things, I would look around me for those who are succeeding and do as they have done."

Achievers must learn to do things they don't want to do. Discipline plays an important part in achieving success. William James advised: "Everyone ought to do at least two things each day that he hates to do, just for practice."

Aldous Huxley said: "Perhaps the most valuable result of all education is the ability to make yourself do the thing you have to do when it has to be done, whether you like it or not."

The Eighty-Twenty Law Is Universal

The principle of mediocrity applies at any level of achievement. For this reason it is always useful to ask oneself: "Am I patterning myself after the average person at my level?"

I hope that my contribution to this book will help at least one eighty-percenter move into the twenty-percenter group. No person who reads this book can say he was never exposed to the philosophy of success.

A Native American legend says all this in a different way: A boy found an eagle s egg and he put it in the nest of a prairie chicken. The eagle hatched and grew up with the prairie chickens. The eagle learned to do what prairie chickens do—scratch for food and fly short distances with a great fluttering of wings. He learned to cackle like a prairie chicken.

In the course of an uneventful life, the eagle grew

old. One day he and his prairie chicken friend saw a beautiful bird soaring on the currents of air above the mountains. The eagle said to his prairie chicken friend, "I wish I could fly like that. What kind of a bird is that?"

The prairie chicken answered, "That's the golden eagle, the king of all birds. Don't give it another thought—you couldn't ever be like him."

And the eagle didn't give it another thought. He died thinking he was a prairie chicken.

My friend, you, too, were born an eagle! The good Lord intended you to be an eagle, *so don't listen to the prairie chickens!*

Dr. RICHARD BENCE

Dr. Richard Bence, from Milwaukee, Wisconsin, is a dentist, a college professor, an investor, a businessman, an author, and a public speaker.

He is engaged in a group practice limited to endodontics. He received his Doctor of Dental Surgery Degree from Marquette University School of Dentistry in 1968 and a Certificate of Specialty and a Master's Degree in Oral Biology from the University of Loyola School of Dentistry in 1972. He has taught anatomy and endodontics at two universities and is an associate clinical professor at Marquette.

Dr. Bence has been involved in several small businesses. In 1977 he developed a special interest in real estate and became a licensed real estate broker and a licensed real estate securities salesman. He is the president of the Richard Bence Realty Company.

Dr. Bence has published more than 30 articles and is the author of a dental text that is used in universities throughout the world. This text, *Handbook of Clinical Endodontics*, now in the second edition, has been translated into French, Italian, Japanese, and Spanish.

His favorite speaking topic is "I Can Do It!" Having learned this philosophy from others, he feels that it must be shared with others. Audiences throughout the Midwest have heard his realistic approach to overcoming the many obstacles which stand between each of us and success. He has also lectured on real estate investments.

As a speaking representative of the Americal Dental Association's Public Education Program, Dr. Bence has made appearances on radio and television.

Dr. Bence has served in the U.S. Air Force as a dental officer, holds a private pilot's license, and is a certified graphoanalyst. He enjoys the pastimes of tennis, sailing, travel, and reading, which he claims are all made possible by the philosophy "I Can Do It!"

Dr. Bence can be contacted by writing to 2040 West Wisconsin Avenue, Milwaukee, WI 53233. Telephone (414) 933-1700.

I CAN DO IT!

by Dr. RICHARD BENCE

I had considered calling this chapter "You and Your Future," but instead I chose the words that have inspired me to try harder on more than one occasion when I've been tempted to quit. They are the words of a five-year-old girl who overcame seemingly insurmountable odds to stay alive and then went on to achieve goal after goal that others believed were beyond her reach. I've never heard anyone so excited, so ecstatic, to reach a goal. A little later I will tell you the story that prompted her to shout out these words: "I can do it! I can do it!"

You, too, can accomplish any goal you set. All you have to do is put your mind to it. I believe that regardless of our ages or past accomplishments, we all have dreams we can claim and goals we can attain by taking positive steps to achieve them.

227

You Can Accomplish the Impossible

It has been said, and I've certainly found it to be true, that that which seems to be impossible is accomplished by doing one almost impossible thing at a time. Jim Bouton had a dream and accomplished the impossible. Jim was a retired major league pitcher for the New York Yankees. His dream was to once again pitch in the major leagues. After laboring for a time in the Atlanta Braves farm system, he was called up to the Braves in September 1978. At age 39, after nearly a decade as an ex-major leaguer, he had accomplished his goal.

Long before Abraham Lincoln was president, at a time when he was too unpopular to retain his seat in Congress, he believed in the abolishment of slavery. He proclaimed that he could never be a slave or master; he believed that this country could not exist with slavery. His reliance on the political principles of our founding fathers prompted him to fulfill the written promise of freedom and equality so clearly stated in the Declaration of Independence. He *believed,* and he achieved.

Throughout the history of the world, people have sought wealth but few have acquired it. Why? Is the successful person *born* to succeed? Why is it that some people succeed in their business and personal lives; while others seem destined to failure? Why do only 5 percent of the people in this country become financially independent?

At age 20 nearly everyone believes he will be successful. The reason so few people succeed is they lack the two factors absolutely necessary to attain wealth: It is essential to have a *definite plan* for self-improvement and an *unwavering obsession* to improve one's circumstances.

Too many people want to improve their circumstances *but neglect to improve themselves.* How many times have you heard someone say "I wish I were in that position—I'd ..," or "If I had $100,000, I'd ..."? They continue to wish without enabling themselves to achieve that desire, so it remains forever just an idle thought.

Notice that doers say, *"When* I am in that position, I'll ...;" *"When* I have $100,000, I'll ..." If you ask them what they are doing to acquire what they want, they will tell you in detail.

Bobby Knight, University of Indiana's controversial basketball coach, explained it this way: "Everyone has the will to win, but to be victorious one must have the will to *prepare* to win."

Have a Game Plan

Most people have only general desires—no specific goals. If I wanted to be a better golfer, I'd plan to break 90 by August and break 85 by the following August. I'd set very specific goals—daily goals—to achieve that objective. I'd take a lesson every Tuesday and Thursday. I'd practice at the driving range every Monday and Wednesday, and I'd arrange to play at least twice a week. I'd prepare for each session by writing down my goal for that day and work hard to achieve it.

The fact of NASA's deciding to place a man on the moon didn't make it happen. When President Kennedy and the country's leading scientists decided to send a man to the moon and back within ten years, they developed a plan. It involved definite and specific goals, checklists, and a round-the-clock work schedule. Their goal was specific, and so was their schedule. It was a race against time. It was a $25 billion adventure.

In July 1969, after eight years of transient triumph

and recurrent despair, Neil Armstrong set foot on the moon and the goal was won.

Few people realize that their dreams come true only when those nebulous and abstract thoughts known as desires are *transformed into action*. Without specific goals we wander aimlessly. Twenty years ago, as a youth, I heard a motivational recording by Earl Nightingale. He spoke about goals and the secret of success. I was so fascinated that I played it over and over again.

To make his point, Nightingale described a ship sent out to sea with a captain, a crew, and an appointed destination. He explained that in 999 chances out of 1000 that ship would reach its destination at a predetermined time. Then he said to consider the same ship without captain or crew or destination. If you were to push that ship away from the dock it would most likely end up on the rocks along some shore—if it got out of the harbor at all.

That example continues to remind me that *we must chart our lives* if we expect to get out of the crowded harbor of mediocrity. We must continually ask ourselves: "What is my destination for one year from now?" "Where would I like to be in ten years?" "Did I plan ten years ago to be where I am today?"

It is inconceivable to me that so many people believe they can reach a destination that they cannot describe *or even name!* It's evident to everyone who succeeds that we need a game plan. That's our reservation to be among those who prosper.

Yogi Berra once said (in a way that only he can): "If you don't know where you're going you may wake up and find yourself someplace else."

Set Deadlines

Besides a game plan, we need deadlines. The most intelligent person alive cannot achieve a goal without a clear and realistic plan. We must make a habit of asking ourselves: "What will I accomplish this week or this day?" "Do I have a well-conceived and detailed plan?"

In my family we have a system to help define and accomplish our goals. We have what is known as the *master list*. On it we enter our plans (both social and financial), places we would like to go (the kids usually write in Marriott's Great America or the drive-in), and jobs that need to be done (repairs, clean-up, or redecorating). Each month items are removed from the master list and placed on a schedule to be accomplished that month. Each week items are removed from the monthly list and placed on a weekly list. And, yes, *each day* items from the weekly list are placed on a daily list. The long-range goals are divided into subgoals to make certain they are achieved.

Everybody has goals, but most people don't write them down. Consequently their goals are forgotten. If keeping a list of your goals seems too structured or time-consuming, try it for awhile. You will find out that it is, in fact, a timesaver. When you see for yourself how much more you accomplish, you will soon be convinced that even day-to-day activities must be planned.

I encourage you to think right now of something you would really like to accomplish in the next year. Write it down and put it where you will see it often—maybe on your desk or on the sun visor of your car. During the next few days plan how you will accomplish that goal.

Use Verbalization

Verbalization is a valuable aid to goal achievement. When you have selected a goal recite it aloud at least once a day. Crystallize it in your mind. Mention it in conversation. When your goal becomes a part of your thoughts and actions you will begin to behave as though it were impossible to fail. And when the people around you know about your goals, you're committed.

Jimmy Carter became president that way. He went around the country saying, "My name is Jimmy Carter; I'm going to be your next president." (He didn't say, "Hi, I'm Jimmy Carter and I *think* I'd like to be president."

Abraham Lincoln gave the following advice to a young law student: "Always bear in mind that your own resolution to succeed is more important than any other one thing."

As soon as you have accomplished one goal, select another. At this point you may be so enthusiastic that you arrange your schedule to include two or three goals, each one scheduled and destined to be achieved. The reason I'm telling you this story about goals and accomplishments is that I want you to feel the thrill of success just as I have.

Dizzy Dean once said, "If you can do it, it ain't braggin'." There is a big difference between a braggart and a determined, goal-oriented individual. I have a wall full of diplomas, certificates, and plaques in my study, but anyone standing in the doorway looking into the room won't see them. They are on the same wall that the door is on; they are for *me* to see. I need that kind of reinforcement if I'm going to move on to accomplishing bigger goals.

To me, achieving a goal is exciting. I know I'll have to pay a price to accomplish big goals, but I'm accustomed to that. H. L. Hunt, one of the richest men in the world, simplified my thinking about goals when he said, "Decide what you want to do or be; then decide what you are willing to give up to get it."

Keep an Idea List

The master list I described to you earlier is in reality an idea list. Each of us comes up with several hundred ideas each day. Most of these are relatively unimportant and don't require any action on our part. But a few of them bring out the genius in us—and these should be acted upon. I keep an index card and a pen in my pocket to write down each idea that comes to me. Later in the day I decide which ideas should be entered on the master list to insure that they are carried through to completion.

About a year ago, I was listening to David Hartman interview an active, successful 102-year-old man on the *Good Morning America* program. Hartman was asking him about his habit of carrying an index card to make note of his ideas. When asked if he had a card with him at that moment, Mr. Jones said: "You bet your sweet life I do!"

For more years than most of us have been alive, Mr. Jones has known the value of recording his ideas—not as a diary, but to keep his mind trained to think. Someone once asked George Bernard Shaw what books he would take with him if he were to be marooned on a desert island. Mr. Jones's answer probably would have been the same as Shaw's: "Blank notebooks."

If you write down your ideas you will be amazed at all the really good ideas you come up with. You will learn to respect the infinite capacity of your mind. And with practice your ideas will get better. As Oliver Wendell Holmes once said: "Once the mind is stretched by a new idea, it will never again return to its original size."

All the breaks we need to succeed are within our own minds. The mind is our greatest security. Its powers are limitless. Napoleon Hill states: "There are no limitations to the mind except those we acknowledge."

We each have a right and a duty to pursue our ideas, to claim them as our own, to be proud of them, and to act on them. Then good things will begin to happen to us. We must not permit others to come between us and our ideas!

In the 15th century Leonardo da Vinci shocked people by predicting that someday men would travel by air. Hundreds of years later people laughed at the Wright brothers' attempts to fly. So don't be embarrassed if people laugh at your ideas!

In order to see an idea through to its physical completion, we must picture it in our minds. The successful saleswoman sees herself writing a big sale. The arm-chair athlete sees himself running a four-minute mile. W. Timothy Gallwey discusses these mental projections in his book *The Inner Game of Tennis.* He emphasizes the need for a clear visual image of the results we desire. He believes as I do that we must unleash the potential within us; that we are designed to succeed. No one can be successful without believing that. Success is an inside job. We do it to ourselves, and we do it by believing.

Generate Enthusiasm

In order to get started on the road to success, we must first overcome apathy. We must do something, *anything,* to get started. Once we've made the commitment, we must generate enthusiasm.

A famous psychiatrist once stated that successful people are decisive. They say one of three things when asked a question: *Yes, No,* or *Wow!*

To be successful we must overcome the human frailty known as procrastination. The opposite of action, it is inertia or motionlessness. Overcoming it is work, but we can't just sit on our hands and wait for something we want to happen.

More than once I've had my car stuck in our Wisconsin snow. But when my children wondered aloud if their dad was stuck, I'd invariably answer, "No, not yet—not until I can't rock the car back and forth anymore." For so long as there was motion, even the oscillatory movement created by moving the car a few inches forward and backward, I wasn't stuck. The trick was never to lose that momentum, because I would then have to overcome inertia. And it is the same with our goals. Once we get started on them, *we must not lose our momentum.* Fortunately it takes less effort to keep moving toward a goal than it does to get started on one.

One of the best ways to overcome the inertia that prevents the realization of our dreams is to set aside just 15 minutes each day to work on goals. (That adds up to less than two hours a week.) I've experienced the value of doing that. Initially I committed myself to getting away from everyone and everything for 15 minutes each day. I found that time so productive that soon I was allocating two or three times as much time.

While watching a televised game during the past football season, I tried to estimate how much time the coaches and players had spent during the previous week preparing for that game. Taking into account the scouting, film review, strategy sessions, practices, and so on, I believe that my estimate of 50 hours of preparation was conservative. Fifty hours of preparation for one hour of playing time! How much time do you think the average person devotes to planning his entire future?

Can you imagine the result if each of us became just ten percent more productive this year than we were last year? That's an improvement of less than one percent per month. Corporations do it. It's essential for maintaining their competitive growth. If we became just ten percent more productive in each of the next ten years, we would be *twice as productive* as we are now. And if we were satisfied with last year's output, increased productivity would allow us to work every other day, or every other week, or vacation for six months of each year! Look around—many people have done it.

Eliminate the Negatives

Once you start a program of goal fulfillment, eliminate any negative or conflicting factors. Eliminate thoughts that could sabotage your objective. I don't allow the words *I can't* in my home. It's better to say (and believe) "I may not be able to do this now, *but I soon will be able to*" or "I'll find someone who can do this for me."

Negative thoughts keep us from concentrating on our goals. They become a self-fulfilling prophecy. If we *believe* we can't do something, then we probably can't. If we listen to people who speak in negative terms, it may cause our thinking to become negative. *Don't deal with negative people*—they are looking for companionship in their thinking. Deal with realistic, positive thinkers and become their companions. Invariably, they are happier and more successful people.

When you select a realistic and practical goal, picture it clearly in your mind, focus your thoughts on it, and become enthusiastic about it. Divide your large goals into sub-goals which will demonstrate your progress and develop your confidence. Soon you will be known as an overachiever in a world of underachievers.

Attaining your goals is such a good feeling that successful people never stop setting goals. In time they become just as successful as they make up their minds to be.

Some people disagree with me about negativism and are quick to point out that it's foolhardy to avoid thinking of certain negative aspects of any undertaking. I agree to an extent. I recommend listing both the positive and negative considerations of any proposed goal, then eliminating the negative points, one by one, so only the positive points remain. Then *never go back to the negative thoughts!*

One of my brothers is a successful home builder who starts each project with a plan or blueprint and finishes with a building that fits the precise specifications of the blueprint. His job is to determine the exact sequence of events that must take place to arrive at the finished project and then expedite it.

His blueprints do not contain any negative statements. Nowhere does it say "Do not construct the room ceilings at a height of six feet." All of the specifications are positive statements, and they are all that is necessary.

It is the same with our minds. It is demoralizing and a waste of time to continually dream up problems when we plan our goals.

The approach I have described in this chapter is not easy to accomplish. But if you work at it, so that it becomes a way of life, it will become easier. Don't tolerate indifference the way 95 percent of the people in this country do. I refuse to tolerate either indifference or procrastination. There is a note on our refrigerator door at home that says "Do it now!"

Starting today, think of your future as never before! Think of the things you want to do. Make your goals your priority. Write down your goals and map out a plan to accomplish them. Then follow that plan to the letter. Most importantly, believe in yourself and expect to succeed. Then you will become the person you want to be. *Don't leave your future to chance!*

•

Now, I'm going to tell you the story that has so often inspired me to try even harder when I didn't think I had it
in me to continue. It's the story I alluded to at the beginning of this chapter. It begins on May 23, 1970, with the
birth of a baby girl. Two weeks later while I was on a
business trip, I called home and was told that this little
baby had developed a fever. The next morning she was
hospitalized with spinal meningitis.

She had been admitted to McConnell AFB hospital,
but at noon she was transferred to the pediatric clinic at
St. Joseph's Hospital in Wichita, Kansas. Her condition
was critical, and she was not expected to live through the
night. During the next 18 hours I drove the 1200 miles to
Wichita. She was still alive.

My daughter had convulsions for five days, during
which she was given enormous dosages of antibiotics.
When she was dismissed from the hospital three weeks
later the neurologist and the pediatrician stated that she
most certainly had suffered brain damage.

By the time she was three years old it was obvious
that this delightful little girl was of normal intelligence.
However, she experienced difficulties with motor coor-
dination and had diagnosable learning disabilities. She attended a school for children with learning disabilities for
the next six years and is presently in the public school
system's LD curriculum.

With that background information, I want to tell you
what this girl accomplished in the spring of 1976. Nearly
three months before her sixth birthday she came to me
and said, "Dad, take the training wheels off my bicycle—
I'm going to learn to ride without them before my
birthday."

Nearly every day she did what I am asking you to do,
that is, set aside 15 minutes a day to work on your goals.
Day after day she sat on that bicycle, moving it back and

forth on the driveway, tipping it from side to side, trying to balance it. One day, a month or so after the training wheels were removed, I watched her from the window. I concluded that she was not likely to accomplish her goal.

But, much to my surprise, she came to me a few days later and said, "Dad, get some film! Tomorrow I'm going to ride that bike, and I want you to take a picture of me."

I had recently bought a sound movie camera, and I want you to know what I captured on that film. We took the bike over to a neighbor's driveway, which had a slight incline. And that almost-six-year-old girl coasted down the driveway and then began to pedal. As she came past me with her face full of excitement and exhilaration, she shouted out in a voice that was partly laughing and partly crying, "*I can do it! I can do it!*"

INTRODUCING
THE SERIES EDITOR:
DONALD M. DIBLE

Don Dible presents more than 100 speeches, seminars and workshops a year all across the United States under the sponsorship of universities, trade associations, chambers of commerce, business magazines, professional societies, and private companies.

His lucid, enthusiastic, experience-backed presentations are designed to inspire and motivate seminar participants and convention audiences to put to immediate use the highly-practical information he covers.

In preparing his talks, Don draws from a rich and varied background. He received his BSEE from MIT and his MSEE from Stanford University. Prior to launching his first business in 1971, he served in engineering and sales management capacities with three companies, including a subsidiary of the SCM Corporation, where he was responsible for directing and training a large national sales organization producing millions of dollars in sales annually.

241

In the past seven years, Don has founded eight successful businesses in the publishing, advertising, seminar, graphic arts services, and real estate industries. All but one of these companies was started on a part-time basis with modest capital resources. Each of Mr. Dible's businesses reflect the unusual and innovative approach he takes to sales, marketing and finance—topics discussed in detail during his many seminars and talks.

While Don is still blazing new trails in his speaking career, he is perhaps best known for his work in the field of publishing.

Prior to writing his 100,000-copy bestseller, *Up Your OWN Organization!*, Don had never written a single word for publication in his life. Aside from writing themes, book reports, and term papers in high school and college, his only major writing project was a highly technical undergraduate thesis at the Massachusetts Institute of Technology.

After working for seven years in industry, Don became frustrated with the rigidly structured world of big business. He looked longingly and lovingly at the outside world of entrepreneurship—and decided to launch his own business.

Following three years of research, including attendance at numerous seminars, interviews with hundreds of successful small business owner/managers, and a thorough review of the small-business books in print at the time, (mostly dry-as-a-bone textbooks and rah-rah get-rich-quick books), he finally decided that the most needed new product in the marketplace was a *realistic* book about starting a new business. Faithful to his commitment, he raised the needed capital; and with the assistance of his dedicated wife he started The Entrepreneur Press. Next he hired a secretary, and in just four months produced a 750-page manuscript for *Up Your OWN Organization!*, with an introduction by Robert Townsend, former Chairman of the

Board of Avis Rent-a-Car and bestselling author of *Up The Organization.*

Shortly after the publication of his first book, Don was asked to assist a professional society in organizing and presenting a two-day conference utilizing the services of fourteen attorneys, accountants, business consultants and financial executives. The program was recorded, the recordings were transcribed, and he edited and adapted the transcripts into manuscript form. The resulting book was *How to Plan and Finance a Growing Business.*

As a result of the success of The Entrepreneur Press, Don has published the following books: *Up Your OWN Organization!; How to Plan and Finance a Growing Business; Small Business Success Secrets: How to Zap the Competition and Zoom Your Profits With Smart Marketing; How to Make Money in Your Own Small Business; Fundamentals of Record-Keeping and Finance for the Small Business; What Everybody Should Know About Patents, Trademarks and Copyrights; Business Startup Basics; Techniques and Strategies for Effective Small Business Management; Profitable Advertising Techniques for Small Businesses;* and *How to Make a Fortune in Import/Export.*

Recently Don founded a new publishing enterprise, the Showcase Publishing Company, dedicated to multi-author motivational and inspirational self-help books. This is the sixth volume published by this company.

Finally, Don has been a guest on scores of television and radio talk shows, including NBC's *Monitor,* with Bill Cullen, and ABC's award-winning *Mike Wallace at Large.* He is also a frequent contributor to magazines such as *Dun's Review, Success Unlimited, MBA Magazine, Free Enterprise,* and *Boardroom Reports.*

You may contact Don by writing to him at 3422 Astoria Circle, Fairfield, CA 94533; or by telephoning (707) 422-6822.

This book was designed & produced
by George Mattingly, at GM Design, Berkeley
from Trump Mediaeval & Friz Quadrata types
set by Robert Sibley, Abracadabra, San Francisco
and was printed & bound by R.R. Donnelley & Sons
Crawfordsville, Indiana.